DON'T FIGHT MAD

A Black Belt's Quest to Recapture Joy

CINDY VILLANUEVA

To my children: Rebecca, James, Alex, and Tristan
With love, admiration, and respect. You are the best of me and I am
grateful for your wisdom and love.

To Great Grandmasters Ernie Reyes Sr. and
Tony B. Thompson
Thank you for inspiring and coaching me to be more.

CONTENTS

ALSO BY CINDY VILLANUEVA

Finding Our Wings: Seven Entrepreneurs

on Reclaiming Hope and Power

FOREWORD

We all start out well, don't we?

We're eager to learn, open to new experiences, quick to take risks. Who hasn't smiled watching a little girl wriggle out of a parent's arms as she yearns to walk by herself, unfettered by the hand of an adult? She doesn't worry about the distance, the hardships she might face, the dangers lurking ten steps ahead. She simply longs to be free, fully confident in her ability to "Do it myself!"

I've been that little girl. So have you.

But somewhere along the way, we lost that confidence. We lost the beautifully reckless will to *do it ourselves*—to jump, skip, run into the unknown, certain that we were fully capable of finding joy just around the next corner. Perhaps it was simply the ordinary ups and downs of life that did it. Or perhaps someone told us early on that life isn't safe and risk-taking is far too dangerous—courageous living just isn't for us.

For some, it has been later in life that we learned our lesson. Maybe it was a divorce—the end of something sold to us as "until death do us part." Something happened that rocked us and told us, "Don't trust, don't risk."

Perhaps it was infertility, the monthly grief that destroyed confidence. Or the death of a loved one that stripped us of support and balance. Maybe you lost a job—and with it, your identity and autonomy. Perhaps a child has gone far astray, breaking your heart and wrapping you in fear.

Or maybe you just made a big, big mistake. One that has had long lasting, devastating effects.

Life abounds in ways to derail us.

I've been there, too. I've had my legs kicked out from under me many, many times. Bullying, domestic violence, adultery, death, and financial catastrophe. I've felt the utter and complete loss of purpose and identity—the anguish that explodes in gut-wrenching screams behind the wheel of my car, stopped in a parking lot by the lake. The deep grief that seems it will never fade, the belief that the pain I feel today will be the pain that haunts and hounds me forever. The ever-present notion that I am to blame for everything, accompanied by the inability to forgive myself.

In this book, you'll learn a bit about me: I'm a martial artist, a seventh-degree black belt school owner. I'm also a mother. Three children came from my body: Rebecca, James, and Alex. A fourth child, Tristan, is a precious bonus that was part of a package deal with my second husband. As a stay-at-home mom, I started martial arts in 1994 as something fun to do with my children. Now, I'm an author, speaker, small business owner...and a woman with a story.

This book tells my story and the stories of people I know—but it's so much more. It's the story of every woman who has faced tragedy and heartbreak, devastation and demoralization, shame and defeat. And it's a story of perseverance, tenacity, and faith. A story of lessons learned, victories won, and fresh starts realized.

It's not a quick-fix. I'm on a lifelong journey to reclaim my *self*...mind, body, and spirit. This is a story of grit and determination, but also grace and love.

You might have picked up this book because you're a martial artist—maybe even a black belt. On the other hand, maybe the thought of sweating makes you break out in hives. Either way, reading the stories and working through the questions at the end of each chapter in Section Two will give you new insight into your life. Fighting may seem like an odd metaphor, but I think you'll be amazed at how closely it aligns to our most profound experiences. Through this book, I hope you'll learn where you've given away or been stripped of your power, autonomy, and joy. And it will help you recapture them through seven steps, allowing you to recover that sense of wonder, eagerness, and openness to taking chances. You don't have to be a black belt to deserve that life.

I want to become that openhearted little girl again—this time, with a woman's perspective. And if you're tired of sitting on the sidelines and are ready to experience a reinvigorated, joyful life, I hope you'll join me.

WARMING UP

Section One

THE BUILD UP

In 1960, the idea that a white woman would marry a Mexican man was ludicrous. Discrimination was firmly entrenched, even in liberal California. These were the days when "No Mexicans Allowed" signs were common. Yet my parents defied common wisdom—including both their families—and married. And in 1961, they welcomed me into the world.

When they snuck out of Corcoran in central California to avoid my maternal grandmother's wrath, they initially headed for Washington State, where my mom's cousin lived. After a short while, they realized it wasn't the place for them. My father, who had grown up as a migrant farm worker, suggested San José. "I remembered it was a nice place we used to go to pick plums when I was a kid," he told me. And so off they went, driving south to what would one day become Silicon Valley.

Life wasn't easy. My mom got pregnant and they began looking for a home big enough for them and a new baby. While my dad was at work one day, she went to look at a duplex for rent. It was perfect and my mom told the owner that she would like to bring my dad to see the place when he got off work. The woman agreed to meet them there later that day. I'm sure she was delighted at the prospect of having such a friendly tenant as my sweet mom.

Cindy with her mom, Carole

When my parents arrived that evening, things abruptly changed. Opening the door, the woman took one look at my dark-skinned father and my obviously pregnant Anglo mom and immediately exclaimed, "There will be no half-breed children in this house," and slammed the door in their faces.

It wasn't an uncommon experience in those days.

Eventually, my parents purchased their own home. A tidy little house with a detached garage, a yard big enough for a swing set, and a garden full of beautiful flowers. Hydrangeas lined the driveway to the detached garage along with a big lilac tree that produced the fragrant blossoms ever-present in vases around the house. That fragrance still says "home" to me.

So that was my beginning. Parents who were strong enough to flout tradition. A father who worked two and sometimes three jobs so my mom could stay home and raise my younger brother James and me. A perfectly kept home, a well-manicured yard, and love—so much love.

My brother and I recently took a boxful of old home movies and had them digitized. It's been delightful to watch them—although a little bittersweet when I see my mom, who died from cancer in 2011. But there's one thing that leaps out at me as I watch them: I am constantly running in circles, laughing, simply full of joy. It's as if there's so much joy in me, I can't stop moving. Movie after movie shows me at three, four, five years old, just running and laughing.

That exuberance sobers me.

Cindy with her brother, James

The older I get, the more I realize how very special my upbringing was. We didn't have a lot, but we were a family. My mom loved to cook and she started teaching my brother and me at a very early age. I remember sitting on the counter, mixing cookie dough. When we were older, one of our special Christmas events was making holiday cookies and bread. My brother and I each got to invite one friend over for the day and we'd make and decorate Christmas cookies. We had a dozen different cutouts—Santa, a star, a snowman, a candy cane. We made red dough, green dough, and regular sugar cookie dough and then frosted and covered them with sparkles or piped icing. It was the highlight of the school vacation each year.

Another of our favorite things was when my dad would say, "Let's go for a drive." We'd pile into the car and just... drive. I didn't know at the time that was because we couldn't afford anything else. It was just fun to be with my parents and my little brother—and sometimes, we'd even get to go to the drive-in A&W Root Beer where we'd order root beer floats. Or we'd go out for ice cream, where my father would always order fresh peach. I'd get to sit on his lap in the parking lot and we'd pretend I was driving us to the moon. Some of my earliest memories are of that huge steering wheel and the fantastic voyages we'd dream up.

My father had big dreams for us. He'd had to drop out of school in the eighth grade—not because he wanted to, but because his parents insisted he quit. As migrant farm workers, his family needed every able-bodied child out in the field, picking cotton, fruits, and vegetables just to keep the family alive. At ten years old, his job was to hold up the flag at the end of the rows of vegetables so the crop duster would know where to fly...and where to spray the poisonous pesticides that frequently caused birth defects in the Mexican babies born in the camps.

But my dad was a rebel. He refused to believe that living in the labor camps was all there was for him and he made his way to Los Angeles, finding work wherever he could.

Having been born just north of the Mexico/United States border meant he was a US citizen, and that meant eventually he was drafted into the Army. He spent two years in Korea, his skinny body suffering through the completely unfamiliar freezing winters, working as a mechanic on Army trucks.

True to his relentless drive, however, he would later use the GI Bill to go to San José State University. "I was not going to get anywhere without an education," he told me. "I was just this dumb Mexican kid, scared to death to speak up, but I couldn't let that stop me." Despite his shyness, he sat in the front row of every one of his classes and set himself the goal to ask at least one question in every session —sometimes simply asking the professor to repeat a statement, just so he could meet his objective. His dream for my brother and me was simple: education, education, education. My mother had graduated from high school but had gone straight to work afterward. She, too, stressed the need for us to excel in school and go to college. Their passion for education found a welcoming home in my happy little heart —from the earliest age, I loved to learn, and I loved to please my parents. Getting straight As became the norm and one more reason to run and dance. Plus, we got banana splits for good report cards!

I loved to learn and I loved to teach. At the end of each school year, I'd ask my teacher for left over "dittoes"—the copies of math and vocabulary worksheets we'd used during the year. I'd take whatever they'd give me and use them to play school with my brother over the summer. He was reading before he started kindergarten, all from playing school with his big sister.

My father loved us, but he could be a hard taskmaster. For instance, my dad believed good penmanship was a sign of attention to detail and commitment to excellence. It was one more proof against poverty and ignorance to him and he was determined that our penmanship would be elegant. So we had regular sessions where we had to draw cursive Os over and over on lined paper, making sure the top of each O touched the top line and the bottom touched the bottom line. They weren't to go over or under, and their angle had to be the same each time. We hated every minute of it, but we both have lovely penmanship.

He also challenged our brains. We played memory games at the dinner table where he'd give us a list of ten words to memorize and then we had to tell him what they were at random. When we first learned the game, he taught us a trick: memorize words one through ten, associating them with something easy to remember. One, run. Two, shoe. Three, tree, and so on. Then, on any evening when he gave us the list of words at the beginning of dinner, we associated them with the things we'd already memorized. For instance, if number five on his list was *volleyball*, we knew that five went with hive. We'd close our eyes and picture a bunch of bees playing volleyball in their hive. When he randomly called out five during dinner, we only had to close our eyes, picture what we'd imagined, and we'd have the word. *Volleyball*.

It didn't feel like work. It was family time.

Cindy and her brother, James

Life wasn't idyllic. Both my parents suffered from depression, although I didn't know it at the time. My mother had ten miscarriages before the doctor finally insisted on a hysterectomy. I only learned much later what profound grief she hid from us. When we were very small, my father was obsessed with providing a perfect life for us and was frequently absent because he was working multiple jobs. He was determined that our childhood would be nothing like his, and he worked himself ragged. It seemed he was always leaving: "Taking off, kids!" he'd say, as he hugged us goodbye. My little brother called him "Take Off Daddy."

When I was six, my father got hired at IBM and finally worked a single job with a regular schedule. No more part-time jobs at the cannery or the bakery or the post office. No more swing shift work at the machine shop. Now my dad left early in a suit and tie, working 7:00 am until 3:42 pm, Monday through Friday. Life settled into a predictable routine. And one consistent refrain was the expectation that we would get a good education.

We started swimming competitively when I was 11 and James was nine. I got reasonably good at it, and my parents sent me a few times to a weeklong summer swim camp in Malibu at Pepperdine University. My mom's younger brother was my favorite uncle, and he and my aunt lived in Santa Monica, a short bus ride from the beach. They picked me up from the airport, kept me overnight, and dropped me off at the university at the start of camp the next morning. After camp, I'd spend another day or two with them. They were childless and glamorous. My uncle, who had been an intelligence officer in the Navy during the Vietnam conflict, was a Beverly Hills attorney. My aunt, whom he'd met in Mallorca when he was in the Navy, was from Switzerland. It felt exotic and exciting to have a close relative with such a great accent. They were both brilliant and treated me like an adult. They were long-distance runners and had healthy food in the house at all times. They were about as different from my home in San José as I could imagine. I was certain I wanted to go to Pepperdine University, live in LA, and be just like them.

When it came time to pick a college, I was recruited

from universities all over the country. I had stacks of letters from recruiters and one summer week in 1978, I visited several in southern California, Pepperdine University among them. After talking to me for a bit, the admissions officer asked if I wanted to go for a walk. I loved the campus and was happy to do so.

"You don't want to go here," she told me once we were outside and out of earshot.

Huh?

She explained that the school was very conservative and I would be far better off someplace like UCLA, where I could stretch my wings and truly achieve my goals without any concern about gender inequality. I was shocked but so grateful for her candid advice—UCLA was on my top three list and suddenly leapt to number one. I also visited Loyola Marymount University and Occidental College on that trip, but her words planted an irrevocable seed in my mind.

In the end, I only applied to two schools: Stanford and UCLA. I was keenly mindful of the cost to apply—in 1978, it was $15 to $25 per application, depending on the school. We simply couldn't afford for me to apply to multiple schools, and the truth was, I already knew where I wanted to go. My parents longed to have a child at Stanford, only 30 minutes north of San José, so I applied. I got accepted.

My dad had rebelled decades before, leaving the labor camps of central California for a new life in Los Angeles.

I had my own Los Angeles rebellion: I accepted UCLA.

It was 1979 and I was on top of the world. I was accepted as an honors student at a prestigious university—the one I'd dreamed of attending. I was one of those weird kids—I knew precisely what I'd be doing for the next 18 years: I'd get my degree in Political Science at UCLA, then go back to the Bay Area and attend Boalt Law School at UC Berkeley. I'd have a dazzling career as an attorney, and then at 30 (the youngest allowable), I'd run for the Senate from the great state of California. Marriage? Kids? No thanks. I was on a mission.

What a difference a year can make.

THE CRASH

Life wasn't perfect before I left for college. I'd gotten involved with a boy my junior year in high school, a boy who definitely wasn't someone my parents approved of. Truth was, I knew he was wrong. What drew me to him? By contrast to all my academic success, I was socially inexperienced and sheltered. Most boys my age were intimidated—I seemed like I had it all together, the brainiac with the bright future. I was captain of the swim team, on student council, sports editor of the school paper. But the truth was, I was insecure when it came to boys. I became infatuated with him because he was infatuated with me.

He was from a horribly dysfunctional family—alcoholism and physical abuse that I'd never seen in my house were his everyday experience. I'd never been drunk in my life, never smoked weed—but he did all that pretty much every week, mostly to escape. I was a straight A student, but he barely graduated high school. Once we started having sex, I just assumed we'd be together forever. And so instead of breaking up once I left for Los Angeles, we stayed together. He actually proposed to me before I left—I wasn't even 18!

My mom had cautioned me before leaving home that even though I was a scholastic superstar in my high school, once I got to UCLA and the honors program, I would be just one of hundreds of superstars. I would have to work harder than I'd ever worked. She was right...but I thrived in the environment, soaking up the classes, flirting with the idea of changing my major to linguistics—until I got the most boring professor on the planet in a psycholinguistics class that I dropped after three days. Back to political science, my long-term plans intact.

In LA, I made new friends. My roommate was from Happy Valley, California—an incredibly wealthy enclave an hour north of where I grew up. She had tons of expensive clothes and used cocaine regularly, which I'd never even seen before. We were friendly but didn't hang out together, especially after (assuming I was asleep) she had sex on the floor at the foot of my bed with a guy she met that night at a football game. It was our first weekend on campus and I was shocked—completely out of my element. On the other hand, she introduced me to two girls from her high school and they became my good friends.

I had quit swimming my senior year in high school due to a shoulder injury but decided to give it a try and walked on to the university swim team. I didn't make the traveling team, but I was now practicing with world class swimmers and an Olympic-level coach. My new friends and I made late night runs to the donut shop at the end of Westwood Boulevard, where at 11:00 p.m., they'd sell leftover donuts for ten cents each before closing up the shop for the day. We'd all scrounge up our dimes and head down to the shop for as many as we could afford. I danced like crazy during "Journey Breaks" where we'd crank up the volume on our Journey albums (remember, this was 1979) for ten minutes— we gave ourselves a strict time limit—and danced around the small dorm room, jumping off the beds and the desks to overcome the stress of studying. I sat with my dormmates in the common room watching the USA hockey team at the 1980 Olympics and cheered with the entire school when the Bruins made the Final Four of the NCAA basketball tournament. I cut class to lie out by the pool during an unseasonably hot week in February. I got a part-time job at a clothing store in the Village.

And I stayed with my high school boyfriend. Six months later, I was pregnant.

I had missed my period and went to the Student Health Center for a pregnancy test. This was years before a quick trip to the drug store for a pregnancy stick would give an instant answer. I had to wait 24 hours to get the results.

When I got the call, I was terrified: what would I tell my strict family, the unbelieving family I'd been talking to about my Christian faith for three years? When I became a Christian in my sophomore year of high school, my mother worried I'd joined a cult. She'd finally come to appreciate my newfound faith and had even started coming to church with me before I left for Los Angeles. What would I tell the new Christians I'd been talking to in my dorm for the past six months? How would I explain a pregnancy to the other Little Sisters of Alpha Gamma Omega, the Christian fraternity I belonged to? The woman at the UCLA Student Health Center had the easy answer: It would destroy my life to have a baby now. I should have an abortion.

I was stunned. That sounded so selfish, I stammered. She calmly changed her approach and told me it was better for the baby not to be born to a teenaged mother, that it would be wrong of me to carry to term. She was calm, soothing, implacable. My shock and fear—combined with her relentless arguments—led me to a gut-wrenching decision: I agreed to the abortion and scheduled it for later that day, a Friday. She assured me it was better not to wait and dwell on it over the weekend.

Shaking from head to toe, I was led to the billing office, where I paid $50 for the procedure. A nurse walked me to a waiting room, where she offered me a sedative to calm my nerves. "But," she cautioned me, "if you take this, you can't change your mind. It would damage the fetus." I took the sedative and shivered in the waiting room chair until another nurse called me in.

Alone in the procedure room, I lay on the table, feet in the stirrups, in tears. "God, forgive me...forgive me...please help me. Please get me out of this. Please, God...I'm so sorry...." My whispered prayers continued, tears running into my ears and hair as the doctor entered and began washing her hands at the sink, seemingly oblivious to my distress. Suddenly, I heard a loud voice just behind me, saying one powerful word.

No.

I sat up, stunned, *who else was in the room?* I looked around but found no one behind me. It was like waking up from a dream, abruptly being returned to my senses. I told the doctor that I changed my mind. She angrily insisted that I see my counselor again and left the room. After I dressed, I was ushered into a room with the counselor where she told me lots of women feel unsure about the procedure. She pulled out a model of a uterus and explained to me precisely what would happen, making the assumption I just needed more information. She assured me I could take some time over the weekend and return on the following Wednesday—they just happened to have another opening that morning. All I wanted was to get out of there, so I agreed and scheduled my appointment.

I never went back.

I finished the semester and left school, saying a forlorn

goodbye to the other brainiacs—the ones who hadn't thoroughly bollixed their lives.

My life made a hard U-turn. Once the golden girl of my family, I was now a statistic: the stereotypical Mexican-American unwed teen mother. How many of those girls had I known at my high school? Babies having babies, people opined. My identity crashed and burned—who was I now? Until that moment, *I was what I had accomplished*. And now? A college dropout with no prospects. A loser. My shame was intense. I had left San José just a few short months before, completely certain I'd never be back except to visit. Now, with my identity and confidence demolished, I couldn't imagine a future since the one I'd scrupulously planned had dissolved. So much for the Senate—so much for law school. I couldn't even complete my freshman year of college. No more banana splits for good grades.

And I was supposed to be someone's mother?

I moved back to San José into my old bedroom at my parents' house and tried to figure out my life. My father was furious with me for continuing the pregnancy, my mother so disappointed over my ruined future. I don't know which was worse. I lost every anchor that had kept me stable—my family, my academic career, my faith. I'd lie to my parents and sneak out to see my boyfriend, acting like an immature, rebellious high school kid. I brought nothing but chaos into my environment. And finally, they had simply had enough. I was seven months pregnant and my parents kicked me out.

I remember my father telling me, "It's like I'm watching you barreling down the highway and I know there's a cliff at the end of it. I'm just watching you fly by and I can't stop you." His obvious pain and frustration hurt, but I didn't know how to change the trajectory of my life.

I moved in with my boyfriend. We found a rundown apartment complex with a furnished apartment and desperately pretended to be adults. He got a job at a manufacturing plant. I got work as a secretary. My dad repainted the wooden cradle both my brother and I had started life in; my dad's older brother bought me a beautiful changing table. I set up the nursery in the second bedroom. I clipped coupons and cooked as cheaply as I knew how. At 18 years old, I was still on my dad's insurance policy, so I had excellent prenatal care, faithfully going to my appointments. And in September 1980, five weeks before my due date, I went into labor.

I was uncomfortable sleeping, so when the pain got bad enough, I moved out to the couch in the living room, rolling up a towel behind my back. I fell back asleep, then awoke. I rolled the towel tighter, leaned against the back of the sofa, and dozed. After doing this a few times, I belatedly realized it was happening every five minutes. But wait—my baby wasn't due until the end of October. What was happening? When I called the doctor, he told me to go straight to the hospital.

At the hospital, it was surreal. I was suddenly very much

not an adult.

The baby had flipped completely over and was "foot-presenting breech." At first the nurse thought perhaps the baby's hand was reaching up, but no...it was a foot. My water broke, and they called the doctor. After another quick exam, he told me I would require a Caesarean section. I begged him to wait—surely the baby would turn back around? No, it had to be done now. Things moved quickly then—I had my boyfriend call my parents, and I was whisked away for surgery.

Rebecca was born at 7:17 am. I was nine days shy of turning 19.

In 1980 there were few of the now common treatments for preemies. I saw her for only a brief second—the nurse rushed her to the neonatal intensive care unit almost as soon as she was delivered. She was put on 100% oxygen just to keep her breathing. Over the next nine days, I visited her in the NICU, sitting in my wheelchair and crying over all the wires and tubes in her little preemie body. She had a clear dome over her head that fogged up from the mist helping her breathe. I slid my finger in at the opening around her neck, rubbing a little circle clear so I could gaze at her beautiful face through the plastic.

The NICU nurses gave her a nickname and put a small label on her isolette: *Rambunctious Rebecca.* At six pounds, seven ounces, she was huge for a preemie. They told me she'd have been a 10-pound baby had she gone full term.

Her size was a significant benefit—she slowly needed less and less oxygen to breathe on her own, her little lungs growing stronger every day. Although they'd expected her to be hospitalized for a month, she improved quickly and was released to come home after nine days. It was my parents who picked me up and brought us to my apartment.

Things were strained with my parents—my mom was over the moon at being a grandmother and wanted to be with Rebecca and me all the time. She hated my apartment and the terrible neighborhood.

Things were also strained with my boyfriend. He was still using alcohol and drugs and was utterly unprepared for adulthood, much less parenthood. We fought constantly and, when Rebecca was three months old, he hit me. We were in the kitchen and my head snapped back, striking the corner of the hood over the stove. The metal cut my head and I reached back to find a small puncture. I looked at the blood on my fingertip, horrified.

It wasn't the first time. He'd hit me one time when he'd visited me at UCLA. But at the time, he'd apologized profusely, sworn it wouldn't happen again...we all know the same tired story. At 18 years old, I had believed him. The truth was, I was so shocked, so ashamed, I didn't know how to extricate myself. I had no skills or ability to stand up for myself and just do the right thing—get the hell out of the mess I was in.

But this time he hit me while I was holding my child.

That night, harshly and coldly I told myself, "You may be stupid enough to let him treat you like this. But no way are you putting this precious child in danger." I wish I could say my self-love was sufficient to make the leap, but it wasn't. There was no self and there was no love. Thankfully, I had enough courage to protect Rebecca, so the next day I left. Without a job or any way to support myself, I went back to my parents' home, full of regrets and deep, insidious shame.

I got a temporary job working as a secretary at IBM, going into the restroom at lunch to pump my breasts so Rebecca wouldn't have to drink formula. I filed legal papers to change her last name to mine (I'd originally given her his last name) and to get full legal and physical custody. It took months and money I didn't have—it was grueling and painful, but I knew I had to protect my daughter. I was wracked with guilt but knew this was one thing I could do that wasn't tainted with ugliness and failure.

After I left to protect my child, I knew I had to get back to school; I had to create a life for myself and Rebecca. I enrolled in night classes at San José State and worked as a secretary during the day while my mom babysat. But it was no use: I just didn't have the maturity to juggle parenting, working, and studying. At one point, I got a headache that progressively worsened every day for eight days. I ended up passing out in the shower after a PE class at the university. I went to a couple of doctors, one of whom thought I might have a brain tumor.

It wasn't a tumor. It was a migraine from stress.

I loved my little girl—being a mother was a surprisingly transcendent and beautiful experience. Her smiles lit up my day and I longed to give her everything she needed or wanted. But I was a child myself, and my decision-making apparatus was woefully inadequate. I ended up dropping out of San José State and just working, trying to figure out life. I fought incessantly with my parents, who were certain they knew better than I did how to raise a child. They were right —but they didn't know how to come alongside me with compassion, only judgment. One night I shouted to my father, "I can't do anything right, can I? If I say it's daytime outside, you'll go double check!" He shook his head in utter disapproval. "You're going crazy," he muttered. Maybe I was. I desperately wanted to move out but couldn't afford it and still had no idea who I was or what my future would entail. The old me was dead and gone, and the new me had yet to emerge from the rubble.

My parents had become Christians and had started volunteering at the church I attended, hosting a Bible study for young adults at our home. I didn't attend, but my mom kept asking me to come. She thought it would be good for me to meet some other young people my age. As a young mother, I knew I had virtually nothing in common with them, but I finally agreed. When Rebecca was three years old, I met a young man in the group. He said all the right things—he had dropped out of Bible college but had big plans for his life. He seemed to genuinely care for my daughter, and after several months of dating, we got engaged. People at my church were thrilled—we were the perfect couple.

His family had money and his mother insisted on a big wedding with people coming from all over the country—in spite of the fact that she couldn't stand me. The guest list soon swelled to 300 people. My parents couldn't afford a big wedding, so we ended up scheduling a Friday night ceremony with appetizers and cake afterward in the church hall. My mom fell in love with a dress I hated and I wanted to please her, so I bought it. I found a lovely white dress and a wreath of flowers for Rebecca, as we intended for the two of us to walk down the aisle together—a package deal. My fiancé and I scrabbled together what little money we had and planned a short honeymoon in Carmel. Rebecca and I moved out of my parents' house into a small two-bedroom apartment and I prepared to be a wife.

Two weeks before the wedding, I knew I was making the biggest mistake of my life.

Rebecca had gotten fussy about something and my fiancé got angry. Really angry. He didn't like the fact that I had tried to pacify her instead of disciplining her. I ended up storming out of his house and driving home, shaking with anger. I knew I shouldn't marry him. But at 21, I didn't have the courage to break it off. I was a Christian woman and I believed that with faith and hard work, all would be well. There were people coming from all over the country to attend our wedding. And I'd been raised by a passive mother who never openly questioned my father. I just didn't know how to take a stand for what I knew was right. And when I got pregnant on my honeymoon, it seemed my future was sealed.

I could only vaguely remember the happy little girl I'd once been. I was still running in circles, only now there was no joy.

For fifteen years, I tried. I had two more children, my beautiful boys James and Alex. I worked hard to be a "good wife," but could never seem to manage the whole subservience thing that he demanded. I came quickly to realize our understanding of the Bible diverged dramatically. Our supposed partnership devolved almost overnight into a patriarchal nightmare. In the space of fifteen years, we were in counseling of some sort for at least ten of them. I was lost—there really was no "I" left. My children meant everything to me, but I had nothing else to live for. I was utterly and completely adrift.

I was fortunate in one way: I was able to stay home to raise my children. I no longer dreamed of the Senate—now I just wanted to be the best mom on the planet. I read everything I could get my hands on, listened to older mentors about creative ways to parent that met the individual needs of each of my children. I was determined that there would be no middle child syndrome in my house, and

I would gift the universe with boys who became truly wonderful men. I was room mom, team mom, you-name-it-mom. I listened to them, played with them, taught them to read, and loved them with everything in me. When Alex was eight, James ten, and Rebecca 13, we all began martial arts classes.

And after fifteen years I was divorced. Rebecca had left home by then, but I was still raising the boys, who were then 14 and 12. I'd been a stay-at-home mom for our entire marriage and was facing the need to be financially independent for the first time in my life. Alex begged me to quit working and homeschool him. He hated having me gone every day and it broke my heart to send him off to school in tears. At one of my lowest points (there were many), we were housesitting for a friend of a friend for three months and I got a job working at a printing press shop for my brother's roommate, trying desperately to keep a roof over our heads and food on the table. I hid all the stress and insecurity from the boys and from my family, keeping up the appearance of strength and positivity. I was determined to keep things as simple as possible for the boys, so when I got a new job that required some travel, I had their father spend the night at my apartment so James and Alex didn't have to uproot or change their schedule. On the first Christmas after the divorce, I asked the boys what they wanted to do for the holiday—I was willing to do whatever would disrupt them the least, and was willing to give up my time with them if that was their choice. I was desperate to minimize their pain. They said they didn't want to choose—and so their father spent Christmas Eve sleeping on my couch and I cooked a traditional meal. I would have done anything to make things less difficult for my children.

After a while, my ex-husband sued me for custody of the boys, contending that I was an unfit mother. The truth was, he was tired of paying child support. As a result, I began parenting and acting completely out of fear. I squandered much of the special bond I had with my sons, becoming a shrew of a mother. I was terrified their father would use anything they did wrong, like cutting school or getting bad grades, as evidence in court that I was a failure and couldn't be trusted to raise them. So I nagged and restricted and nagged some more, just when my sons needed my compassion and support most. And when the judge decided that she'd get hyper-involved with our scheduling and gave their father 45% custody, I became even more frantic. I covered a huge white board on the wall with our arcane custody agreement just to remember who went where and when—both boys here or there, one boy here, another there? Two days this week, four the next? It was chaos...and it was maddening.

So much for the golden girl. So much for supermom. There was no running and no joy.

And yet...that wasn't the end of my story.

THE FIGHTER

Today my kids are grown and we have largely repaired the rift my frantic, fear-based parenting caused. It took years of courage: on their part, to be brutally honest with me about their experience and their pain, and on my part, to listen with a vulnerability that often gutted me. We're close and loving and open with each other now. I've learned that it means a great deal to them when I share myself, with all my flaws. They are my biggest cheerleaders and frequently my life coaches. They've shown me how to make transparency and vulnerability a priority in our relationships. They are spread out geographically yet we see each other, talk on the phone, or text several times a week, always keeping in touch. Nothing is more important to me than my kids.

Lots of other things have changed, too. Professionally, I've transformed from being utterly lost to becoming a "multi-preneur." I am the owner and master instructor of Ernie Reyes' West Coast World Martial Arts in Austin, Texas, one of over 40 WCWMA Association schools in the United States. I'm a seventh-degree black belt and I am one of only four woman-owned schools in the Association. In the years I've owned my school, I've graduated dozens of black belts, many with advanced degrees, and my school has received numerous Top School awards for leadership. My students regularly receive Best Tester awards at our semi-annual black belt tests.

I'm also the founder and principal at Knockout Marketing Strategies, a boutique marketing communications agency. I work with small business clients, primarily women, in the Austin area. And I'm an adjunct professor at Concordia University Texas in the College of Business and Communications where I teach both undergraduate and MBA courses. Teaching young minds truly fills my soul.

My life is dramatically different today. I'm no longer that broken, insecure girl.

I've been exceptionally fortunate *and* I've worked hard to make a different life. I went back to school—this time successfully—and completed a Bachelor of Science in Management and Ethics with a minor in Bible and Theology when I was 40 years old. And that parental mantra of "education, education, education" has never left me. I went back again and received an MBA at 50—earning straight As while working full time and teaching at my martial arts studio. I've had the great opportunity to travel all over the world, working in countries as disparate as Japan, the Netherlands, Singapore, Australia, and the United Kingdom, leading global teams of over 100 employees. Since being nearly homeless after my first divorce, I've owned houses in three states. I've been a featured speaker at women's conferences and retreats, and I published my first book, Finding Our Wings, with six other women entrepreneurs.

So how is it possible that my life today differs so dramatically from 1998? How did I go from a single, unemployed mom barely making ends meet to the great life I have today? What transformed me from a woman utterly lacking confidence and identity to a secure and brave leader? The simple (yet not easy) truth?

I learned how to fight.

And I don't mean the Punch-Like-a-Girl pink t-shirt version. I mean the *roll up your sleeves, this is gonna be a brawl, somebody's 'bout to get knocked out, don't mess with me* kind of fight. The kind of fighting that isn't what nice girls do. The fighting most girls aren't socialized to experience. *I learned how to fight.*

You may be surprised that the basics of fighting are a beautiful metaphor for life. Forget about rope-a-dope and "Cut me, Mick!" This isn't about standing eight-counts or Mr. Miyagi and Daniel-san's winning crane kick. This isn't the flippant use of the word "badass" to describe a powerful woman. This is fighting that frees us up to live the lives we were always meant to experience—lives of joy. Ferocious, life-enhancing, transcendent joy. The kind of joy that spills out of you and changes everyone you meet. A joy that builds a foundation for whatever you choose to do, no matter what obstacles you encounter. It's not fireworks and confetti. It's that deep, transcendent joy that means you can take a punch and remain standing. And once you've learned to stand, to fight back and overcome.

There's no sugar-coating the truth: I fell hard for over twenty years. I went from superstar to utter disaster. There were days when nothing but my love for my children kept me alive. I've vomited blood and passed out, cracking my head on the sink due to stress. I've lain facedown on the floor, screaming at God and declaring, "What good are you?" And it's not as if nothing terrible has happened since then. After a ten-year heartbreaking battle, I lost my mom to cancer. I went through a brutal second divorce. I nearly lost my studio. I've had to deal with deep, mind-boggling, heart-rending betrayal. But those things didn't bring me to my knees in the last twenty years; instead, I've been able to face those attacks, bear them, and overcome them. It's my sincere hope that these stories—mine as well as others'— will spark something in you: your inner, hidden black belt. That fighter who transcends tragedy and defeat and finds a way to reclaim joy.

In Section Two, I'll walk through some black belt basics.

The good news is that you don't ever have to get on the mat or put on boxing gloves. You will, however, have to dig deep and train your heart, your mind, and your spirit. You'll have to face your opponent—and sometimes that will be your own self. Nevertheless, no matter what has knocked you down, you *can* earn a black belt in life. And although nobody earns a black belt overnight, it can be done over time. It just takes a relentless commitment to *you*—your health and well-being. I'll share seven imperatives—seven powerful steps to learning how to fight, how to regain your identity, confidence, courage...*and joy*.

It's the joy of that little girl, running in circles and laughing gaily at life. She's me. She's you. Let's go meet her in the depths of our hearts and release her to impact the world.

BATTLING

Section Two

GET IN THE RING

At every martial arts tournament, you'll see the rings set up for competitors. There's plenty of seating around each ring for the spectators—the people who have come to watch and cheer for their favorite martial artists. No one pays attention to the spectators. It's the ones in the ring who are the center of attention. Whether the competitors are four-year-old Little Dragons or black belt adults, the ones in the ring are the stars of the show.

After you've crashed and burned in life, it's much easier (and feels safer) to be a spectator. You sit outside the action, always imagining what could be, what should be. You may torment yourself with memories of being in the ring, of having the courage to fight. But you've learned your lesson and you're not setting foot in there again.

After my first divorce, I got a job writing monthly

customer newsletters for a technology company in California. My brother had worked at the company and introduced me to the hiring manager, a charming woman several years younger than I was. As part of the hiring process, I had several interviews with a number of managers in the Marketing department. They all went well...until one.

Halfway through our conversation, she looked at me with a puzzled expression. "I have to ask you," she said. "Did you just not like school?" I felt my cheeks redden and my heart started to pound. Like school? *I loved school!* My shame at dropping out of two colleges rose up and I wanted to bolt from the room. I took a deep breath and explained that I had left school to have a baby and that I'd taken courses off and on for the past 15 years while raising my family but hadn't completed my bachelor's degree. I barely remember the rest of the interview; I was so frazzled. I felt completely unworthy. What on earth was I thinking putting myself out there? I was certain I'd be rejected. The shame was overwhelming.

Somehow, I got the job.

My confidence was in shreds, and I was just grateful to have stable employment. I enjoyed the work—I've always enjoyed writing—and most of my colleagues were friendly and made the office an enjoyable environment. Nevertheless, my parents' voices constantly rang in my head: *education, education, education.* The manager's question made it crystal clear to me: *I had to finish that degree.* I began looking into returning to college, knowing that my decades-earlier goals were no longer what I wanted. Now, I just wanted the letters after my name, some kind of testimony to not being a failure, some kind of insurance that I could provide a good life for my sons. And so, six months after starting my job, I enrolled in an evening degree completion program at San José Christian College, where they accepted most of my patchwork quilt of credits. It would take me 20 months, but I'd finish with a bachelor of science degree in Management and Ethics with a minor in Bible and Theology. I took out a student loan that made me queasy to contemplate. But finally, I had the maturity and drive to juggle work, parenting, and school. I'd study and do homework after the boys went to bed, just to keep from missing out on time with them.

Over the next year, I had the opportunity to write a lot, both at school and work. At one point, I had moved beyond my role as copywriter. I was on loan to the public relations manager, writing corporate press releases. It was the heyday of the company: I wrote about new products, partnerships, sales, and acquisitions nearly every week. Seemingly from one day to the next, I'd gone from the quiet newsletter writer to the woman knocking on the door of the Chief Financial Officer to get his approval on the latest release. The vice president of Marketing liked my writing style and my calm demeanor in the face of tight timelines and, when the PR manager resigned, he offered me her job. It was a management position, working closely with executive staff, and came with a 40% raise.

I was terrified.

That night I went to class and during a break, I asked to speak privately to my professor. I told her about the new job opportunity and the vastly increased level of responsibility, visibility, and compensation. She looked oddly at me, tilting her head. "And?" she asked.

"I've never been in PR in my life!" I responded heatedly. "I don't know how to do this job!" My professor put her hands gently on my shoulders and said, "Cindy...."

I continued, oblivious to her interruption. "What if I mess it up? What if I can't do it?"

"Cindy...."

"Professor, *I don't have a degree!*" In my mind, there was no more important fact. It was the nail in the coffin of my aspirations.

It had become my identity.

My professor laughed in my face. "Are you kidding me? Take the job." She shook her head and repeated: "*Take the job.*"

That's business-speak for "Get in the ring."

GETTING KNOCKED OUT OF THE RING: CECILIA'S STORY

Years before, I went to high school with a girl I'll call "Cecilia." Cecilia seemed to have everything. She was beautiful, funny, warm, and kind. Beyond everything else, she was fast. As a freshman, she was the fastest sprinter on our varsity track team, an absolute blur in the 100, the "no way we can lose" anchor leg on the 4x100. We became fast friends and hung out constantly, driving around in my 1966 Mustang, thinking we were so cool. We'd talk about boys and music and running, and one Easter, I took her with me to a sunrise church service in the foothills outside San José.

Yet her life was anything but perfect, and I had absolutely no idea.

When Cecilia was very young, her family lived on Long Island. Her mother was pregnant with a fourth child; her father was a professional jazz musician. The three kids all slept in bunk beds they'd gotten from their grandparents, with my friend on the top bunk above her sister.

One night, Cecilia awoke and realized she was in bed with her sister. She got up to climb back into her bed and screamed—there was another girl there she didn't know. Her screams woke everyone in the house and her parents came running in. They brought all the children downstairs where there was another woman waiting—the mother of the unknown girl. Frightened, yanked from sleep and disoriented, Cecilia listened shakily while her father informed everyone that this woman was the "second mother," and that they would all be a family. His secret life was now revealed, and his wife and children were expected to simply accept it.

The family moved to California where Cecilia did everything to escape her home. School became a sanctuary. "The only thing normal was getting on the bus with normal kids with normal families," she told me. Sports became her refuge, one more reason to stay out of her house. She and her siblings were adept at hiding their family life; I never had any idea what was going on in her home.

I was a couple of years older than Cecilia, and we drifted apart when I left for university. Her tragedies, however, continued to mount. Dating became yet another escape, and she became pregnant at 18, dropping out of high school to have her little girl. Her boyfriend vanished, and she found herself on welfare, living in subsidized housing on the worst side of town. She worked on the side while collecting welfare, trying to keep a roof over her head and provide for her baby—and got caught and cited for welfare fraud. She was placed on probation with the constant threat of jail should she ever break the law again.

When her daughter was two, Cecilia met Larry, a man 17 years her senior. A university basketball coach, he seemed stable and loving, and they were together for nine years. She worked hard to improve her life, going back to school and earning two degrees—but keeping still more secrets. Larry was a drug addict and alcoholic, and Cecilia worked hard to keep his addictions from the public eye. Without any family support or self-confidence, "I did everything to keep him," she said.

She had no identity, no power, and certainly no joy. Cecilia was lost—and things only got worse when she was arrested, taking responsibility for Larry's drugs to keep him out of jail. The old welfare fraud citation was dredged up, and Cecilia went to prison. She sent her daughter to live with her sister and began what would end up being eight months in prison before receiving early release into a halfway house.

And then she went back to Larry.

Finally, after nearly two more years, she'd had enough. She was at the end of her strength—as she put it, "There's no way out for me. I'm beyond redemption." Yet out of love for her daughter, she packed up and moved to Fresno, a small city in central California.

She knew that the life she'd led and the things she'd experienced were tragic, and she had little hope for a better future. She clung to her love for her daughter and tried to make a quiet life, well out of the ring.

———

Are you like Cecilia and me, sitting on the sidelines of life? Did you get knocked down and now you are hesitant...terrified...panicked at the thought of reengaging with the world? The slightest challenge makes you flinch, and you've decided that life is now no more than just keeping your head down. The old adage about getting back on the horse sounds like pure nonsense to you—you know what happens when you get back out there. There are no guarantees. No happily ever after. No reset button. You got in the ring at one point in time *and you lost.* And now you've convinced yourself that sitting on the sidelines isn't so bad. There may not be any joy-filled moments, but there's no tragedy either. It's a vanilla existence, but it's safe.

Vanilla's not so bad. You can live with beige, cheese pizza, one-piece bathing suits, and elevator music. It's better than risking it all, right? And no matter what happened to bring us to this point, far too many of us blame ourselves. We cling to the notion—we insist—that we could have done things differently. We could have made better choices, responded in a better way. And when we fall into the trap of holding ourselves solely responsible for our tragedy or trauma, we lower our standards: *this life—this safe, dull life—is all I deserve.*

Instead of processing, healing, and learning, we punish. We deny ourselves the grace we need and deserve, the grace that elevates us and gives us a hand up, into the ring of life.

When we make the decision to sit this one out, to take our place on the sidelines of life, we deprive the world of our talents, our skills, our voice, our vision. Of the unique things that only we can deliver. Nobody shines on the sidelines. We find the lowest common denominator and we forget what it means to excel. And those around us are the poorer for it. No matter what we've been through—no matter what we've done or not done—we have a unique and wonderful purpose in life that simply doesn't get realized when we abandon the ring.

It's not just about you. *Someone in this world needs what you have to offer.*

AND THEN THERE ARE THE JUDGES

Along with the spectators, at every ring there are black belt judges, the ones responsible for scoring the event and deciding who wins and who loses. Some judges are fair; others are not. Some judges are skilled; others are amateurs.

Maybe instead of convincing you to play it safe, your pain has hardened you. You're not getting in that ring—no way! But to avoid dealing with your own pain and shame and *less-ness,* you've become a judge. Your hurt makes you angry, mean, bitter, or unkind. In the fight that is life, it's too easy to become a judge and use the role to bolster our own battered self-esteem to the detriment of others. And grace? What's that?

Perhaps some of these lines sound familiar.

- *She's got a lot of nerve putting herself out there like that —who does she think she is?*
- *Seriously? She's wearing that?*
- *Maybe she's courageous to go back to school, but no way is she going to finish with all those kids to raise.*

- *Isn't she a little old to start martial arts/belly dancing/drumming/acting/fill in the blank?*
- *I'm not surprised her husband left her—look how she takes care of herself.*
- *She must have slept with somebody to get that job.*
- *Yeah, she looks great, but I'll bet she's bulimic.*

And on and on. We may lack the courage to get into the ring. Maybe we believe we're unable to return to the fight. Either way, we find ways to chop down anyone who does. Judging others doesn't feel good—we know it's wrong—but it's better than digging deep and finding the nerve to step out ourselves. Judging others keeps us bound in perpetual comparison that we simply can never win no matter how many people we tear down.

To reclaim our power, identity, and joy we must *get in the ring*. At some point we have to stop making excuses. Stop belittling others who are out there, just doing their best. Stop waiting for the perfect moment: the perfect moment doesn't exist.

Just stand up and get in the ring.

GETTING IN THE RING: CECILIA'S STORY

Cecilia and her daughter settled into a quiet life in Fresno. Resolutely, she rebuilt her life, slowly preparing to reenter the ring. She found a job and began to make friends. And then she met a man—a real man, a kind and loving man. He fell in love with Cecilia, who didn't tell him her story until the day he proposed. She was ready for the ring. But was he?

He didn't flinch. Instead, he encouraged her to continue the fight for her identity, her dignity, her joy. Together, they traveled up to San José where she legally changed her name, in a ceremony designed to put her past behind her. Soon, she married that man and they began a new life.

Cecilia continued her transformation. She walked away from her painful past and refused to sit on the sidelines crushed by guilt and shame any longer. Today she is a pillar in her community, a thriving entrepreneur, and a beloved wife, mother, and grandmother. We recently got to meet again in person, and her glorious, vibrant light just beams. She laughs heartily, hugs readily. As she put it, "I couldn't understand why God would care about me. I should have been dead."

When her grandson was eight years old, he surprised her one day by asking, "Why don't you get baptized? You know you want to." It was the final piece of the puzzle—she was ready to receive a divine gift of love and acceptance. "You don't have to work," she told me, with a smile. "Just believe and there is a beautiful world of hope."

———

Getting in the ring may not be a single action. It may feel close to impossible. It can take minutes or it can take years to step into the ring of life. The important thing is your commitment to getting there. If your pain is recent, it may be all you can do just to get out of bed today. *Give yourself grace.* Put down the credit card. Set down the wine glass. Power walk around the block or get a new haircut. If you've been muddling along for a while, you may be ready to take bigger steps. You may need to change your name or take the damn job. Action begets action, and you'll find that taking baby steps leads to bigger steps. When a fighter comes into the arena, before stepping into the ring, her walk-in music is blaring. What's your theme song?

I really believe that most of life is a math problem. We have to solve for the variables, but that means we have to set up the problem correctly. What do I know? What exactly am I solving for? If we ask the right questions instead of simply reacting, we set ourselves up to be successful. Take some time to genuinely reflect and answer these questions. Be ruthless with yourself: Hedging won't help you but honesty will. Be willing to ask and answer the difficult questions that will spur your walk toward the ring.

Cindy Villanueva, Photo: Marc Morales

ASK YOURSELF

Am I a spectator, a judge, or a participant?

_____

_____

What's keeping me out of the ring?

_____

_____

What am I afraid of?

_____

_____

Whose disapproval am I worried about?

_____

_____

What value is there in staying on the sidelines?

_____

_____

If I've become a judge, how does that serve me?

_____

_____

How can I express grace to myself and others?

_____

_____

Before you know it, you'll take that step into the ring. In the next chapter, you'll consider another step first.

———

GET IN THE RIGHT RING

At the bigger martial arts tournaments, there are dozens of rings. I take my students to the Lone Star Open in Austin each year, and there have been as many as 30 rings, each dedicated to a separate division. At the center of the tournament there stands a raised ring, twice the size of all the others. It's where the black belts compete, surrounded by a boisterous audience screaming their approval after every sparring point scored or impressive vertical side kick in a kata, the traditional form simulating a fight against multiple opponents.

Needless to say, the four-year-old beginners don't spar anywhere near the black belt heavyweight men. When a competitor checks in at the beginning of the tournament, she's given a card for each event she's entered. The card notes the division and ring number. Each competitor must know precisely which ring to enter. In fact, guiding new students to their correct rings is one of the most important things I do at tournaments.

It's one of the most important things you should do, too. Before you get in the ring, make sure it's the right one.

When I tested for my second-degree black belt in 2000, there weren't a lot of women at that level. There were several candidates testing for their first degree, and there were many men at every level. But for some reason, that year there weren't a lot of second-degree women. When it came time to spar, we fought each other, but there weren't enough of us to really test our skills.

One of the senior black belts overseeing the sparring, a fifth-degree school owner from Palo Alto, surprised us all by asking if any of the women were willing to fight the men. At the studio where I trained in San José, we always trained co-ed, but it certainly wasn't the norm for the rest of the Association. Most of the other schools required women to fight women and men to fight men—and ne'er the twain shall meet. At the startling question, every one of the other women stepped back, but my instructor motioned me forward and immediately responded that I would. I had done well in all my matches against the women, but this was a different story. This wasn't training in my studio with my regular male sparring partners—this was our black belt test, and testosterone and adrenaline were running high. Nevertheless, I jumped in enthusiastically.

And got my ass kicked.

I scored a few points, but I just wasn't as strong or big as the men. Their arms were longer and their power was intimidating. Sure, I won bragging rights by being the only woman willing to put herself out there, but I didn't win a single match out of the three I fought. Why?

I wasn't in the right ring.

When you make up your mind to get back in the ring, don't just dive in without thinking. It's essential that you get in the right ring. If the ring is too easy, you'll be bored and unchallenged. Imagine me walking into the Little Dragons ring to spar with four-year-old white belts! It may feel safe and comfortable to jump into an easy ring, especially when you've been knocked out by life, but it will do nothing for your self-confidence or self-respect. Remember, this process is designed to rebuild you, and the too-easy ring isn't going to help. This is where it's essential to seriously and objectively review your entry point. *Yes* to baby steps. *No* to a ring where you'll be embarrassed by your success instead of energized. Be smart about where you reenter life!

Likewise, don't let your pride get the better of you and put you in a ring that's far too difficult. I may have earned the same level of black belt as the guys, but there was no way around their size and strength advantages. I was fast and skilled, but it wasn't enough. When I was in the right ring—the women's second-degree black belt division—it challenged me and required all my skills to be successful. I felt proud and accomplished after each bout, even if I didn't win. I reveled in emotions that built me up and were foundational to my well-being. Even when my opponent scored a point, I knew I was competing well. Putting yourself in a ring outside your weight class can set you back and, especially in the early stages of recovering, you are looking for wins.

Saying yes to life is a win.

We frequently end up in the wrong ring because we've listened to the wrong voices. For instance, we're in the wrong career because our parents' expectations back when we were in college have driven us for years, long after our adult minds and hearts knew we were in the wrong place. We stay in commitments out of duty or obligation or guilt, rather than from a real sense of altruism or calling. When you are ready to get back in the ring, do it right. Listen to the right voices, the voices of those who know, love, and respect you. Most important, listen to your heart—*not your fears*. Where should you be? What lights you up? What lifts your spirits and captures your imagination? If you are a woman of faith, pray—and expect to receive clarity and guidance. My prayer journals have hundreds of entries asking God for clear direction.

In addition to faith, use your intellect. I recommend taking a rigorous inventory of your typical week. Take some time—a couple of hours at least—and write down everything you've done in the past several days—at least four days, and with at least one weekend day. Be as granular as possible, including even mundane things like running to the grocery store or paying bills. Add everything, from quiet time reading a book to staying up until 2 a.m. finishing a project for work, from a retail therapy session online to dinner with a friend. Write it all down. Next, categorize each activity as a "have to" or a "want to." This may not be as simple as it sounds. If an activity is both, then write that down. For instance, I don't enjoy the financial responsibilities of owning a business. I have a CPA, a bookkeeper, and a treasurer, but I still have to stay on top of what's going on in my school. But that "have to" is also a "want to" because I want to be a successful entrepreneur and a good steward of my business.

Once you've categorized your activities, think about how time felt for each one: Were you marking time, checking your watch every few minutes? Or did you lose track of time, surrendering to the joy of whatever you were doing? We all have to do things we don't enjoy and frequently we're astonished that five minutes feels more like an hour. Conversely, when we're "in the zone" or "flow," we can be similarly astonished that hours have passed without us realizing it.

Next, note whether or not you can map each back to a greater purpose. Humans long for purpose. We want to know that what we do really matters. I love the story of President Kennedy taking a tour of NASA and meeting a janitor during the tour. When the president asked him what he did at the facility, the janitor proudly answered that he was sending a man to the moon. Regardless of our activity, if we can map it to a greater purpose, it produces pride and a feeling of accomplishment. An hour of reading curled in your favorite chair with a glass of wine may seem self-indulgent, yet it can truly map back to the greater purpose of self-care.

And last—but most important—write down how it made you feel. Were you energized, captivated, bored, resentful, ecstatic, angry? Be honest and don't judge. You feel how you feel, and right now you are just collecting data.

Once you've collected all the data, it's time to analyze what you've found. Most people find clear trends: the activities that light you up, the ones you can map to a greater purpose and that bring you joy—these are the clues, the event cards, if you will—to which ring is yours.

Keep in mind that, depending on where you are in your healing journey, your ring will look different. Years ago, I was faced with a decision. After 10 years at one company, I was battered. I'd been miserable for years, being disrespected and mistreated, smack in the middle of the stereotypical mean-girl environment. But I'd stayed because I was the breadwinner for my family and the thought of trying to find something else that paid as well when I was in my fifties was daunting. Then I got laid off and, six weeks later, my second husband informed me he wanted a divorce. I learned later that he'd found another sugar mama now that I could no longer provide.

I was on the ropes...and I just walked out. Not just out of the ring but out of the tournament.

I cocooned at a dear friend's lake house in Austin for five weeks. God bless the women who rallied around me! I wouldn't even look at a ring, much less step into one. For the first two weeks, I curled up and refused to take any risks.

The next few months were painful. I was in the middle of training for my sixth-degree black belt, and my soon-to-be-ex-husband wasn't just my business partner, he was my training partner—I didn't have anyone else at my level in my school. While we were testing for sixth degree, the next group of senior students were testing for fourth degree and didn't know my curriculum—they were too busy trying to master their own! The Mastery tests are historically incredibly difficult. Several days long, they are designed to test mental, physical, and spiritual fortitude. They occur every four years because they require over a year just to plan, with students coming to California from all over the country. And for the 2016 test, our grandmaster had completely revamped the curriculum. He told us he wanted his school owners and senior instructors to feel like white belts again, to be able to genuinely empathize with all our students and to have to push ourselves harder than ever before.

And so I was not only trying to understand what the hell

had just happened to me in my marriage, I was training for the most difficult test of my entire martial arts career. Our curriculum is a mixed martial art, with components from tae kwon do, American boxing, Muay Thai kickboxing, Brazilian jiu-jitsu, and Filipino stick and knife fighting. Everything about the 2016 test required a partner—a partner in very, very close range. Imagine doing jiu-jitsu, lying on your back with your legs wrapped around the man who doesn't want to be married to you anymore. It was gut-wrenchingly, soul-crushingly painful. And the couple of times I walked off the mat in tears, he snapped at me and told me not to make a scene at the studio. I turned into a robot, going through the motions, but I stayed at it.

I emailed our corporate headquarters to change my last name, previously hyphenated, on my new black belt and the certificate I would receive after passing the test. A couple of days later, my grandmaster, Ernie Reyes Sr., called me to find out what was going on. I was surprised—with 40 schools across the country and a Mastery test to deliver, he took time to make sure I was all right. We talked for half an hour, and he shared his own story of being a twice-divorced man and how he believed in me and my resilience. He even ventured an opinion that someday I would find a man who would recognize how wonderful I was.

That was the very last thing on my mind.

The tragedy of my second marriage and divorce was compounded by my faith. I became a Christian when I was

15 years old, and while I had not always lived my life according to biblical principles, it remained key to my identity. We attended church weekly—my husband was even the head of security at our church! I had formed a little group of Christian women at the studio who prayed over our school and our students each Wednesday night. I couldn't believe that I was going to be divorced for the second time. Would I ever have any legitimacy as a woman of faith? Would people look down on me for my failure? All I could do was remain true to myself, to refuse to sink to the gossip or the scorned woman bitchiness I knew some people almost wanted to see. I wanted to be an upright woman of integrity, no matter the cost.

Three months passed. I decided that I'd had enough. I started training alone, staying late at the studio or going back at 11:00 at night, turning up the music full blast and working until the sweat ran off my body in rivers. I boxed for rounds and rounds, the ring timer set at three minutes. When my strength flagged, I screamed—literally screamed —"One more round! One more round! *Do not stop!*" I got in the best shape of my life and made plans for my trip to California. I was still unemployed, so I cut every financial corner I could, thankful that I didn't need a hotel room or car during the week-long test.

One afternoon, a black belt mom approached me at the studio. Both her kids had been students with us for years and were now first-degree black belts. She asked if she could talk to me privately, and we stepped into my office. She began to cry. "I'm sorry," she said, brushing off tears, "I don't mean to pry into your business." I realized she was going to talk about the divorce. She took a deep breath and continued, "I just want you to know that I admire you so much—you show so much grace, and you inspire me."

It was my turn to cry.

I couldn't imagine how someone could be inspired by me. I felt sure I inspired pity. But inspiration? I was humbled, touched deeply. My only intention was to get up every morning and look at the woman in the mirror and be proud of how she comported herself. Nothing flashy, not trying to sell anything. I told myself, "I don't have to be Mother Teresa. Just be me." Turns out authenticity and dignity didn't just help me get through the crisis. Others noticed, and they were moved. It became yet another of the profound lessons I would learn through the experience.

I made it to California and began the test. At one point on the first day, my grandmaster's wife, herself an eighth-degree black belt, took me aside. "Kick ass," she told me sternly. "Do you understand what I'm telling you? Kick ass." My single-minded training paid off, and I got through the test in excellent form, receiving numerous accolades—including best physique for my division. My team won many of the challenges that week, and I came home with enough awards to fill a shadow box that I hung prominently at my school.

But I was still wounded and stuck in a business partnership that was beyond toxic.

FINDING THE RIGHT RING: SANDY'S STORY

Years earlier when I was still in California, I trained with Sandy. She was born in 1957 when, as she told me, "Girls should be secretaries, bank tellers, or moms." Sandy was different, though: she loved technology, working with her dad on electronics projects in their garage. Yet after high school, she took classes in 10-key and shorthand, trying to get a "girl's job." She hated every minute of it. Talk about the wrong ring.

In 1977, her brother brought her an application for a job at Hewlett-Packard—a real technology company. Sandy got the job, and began a summer stint in manufacturing, working with "a bunch of old women who did nothing but gossip all day." She held her emotions in check, trying to be happy she didn't have to work as a secretary. But it didn't work. She was miserable.

Finally, she got her chance. A technician position opened and Sandy applied. She went through two three-man panel interviews, and then a third with four men. She lied, telling them she had professional experience in electronics, knowing she could do the job—she knew without a doubt it was her ring.

Sandy got into the program, but it was a fight from the

start. She was the only woman there, but she made it her ring. She became a technician, advancing to level three out of five. "I got to be a very good tech," she told me. "But I got really beat down." Something had to give, and she ended up making "lousy food choices. I would eat for comfort."

Getting into the right ring may not be easy and doesn't guarantee success. But, as Sandy wryly noted, "You bounce back and you learn from your mistakes." Sandy spent 30 years working at HP, grinding it out, determined to make that ring her own. By the time she retired, she was a top technician, well respected and honored. She went through gastric bypass surgery, tamed her eating disorder, and earned her first-degree black belt. She's an award-winning quilter, creating quilts that take months to design and sew. She found her rings and she owned them, through grit and passion.

––––––––

When I got home from the 2016 Mastery black belt test, I knew I had to get back into the ring. But which one? A black belt division ring was beyond my emotional strength. My confidence was still weak, and I didn't have Sandy's courage to attempt anything difficult. I had started a boutique marketing communications agency several months before, but it felt like too much to throw myself 100% into its growth. Instead, I decided to take a job at my university, at 40% of my previous salary. I knew I'd have to take money out of my savings account every month just to make ends meet. It certainly wasn't a black belt ring, but it wasn't a Little Dragons ring either. In the role of director of business partnerships, I had to dust off long unused skills and learn new ones. I had the opportunity to meet and work with amazing people; first among whom was my boss, a brilliant woman who just happened to be the same age as my daughter. It was a Lutheran university, an unfamiliar "high church" environment. I was able to attend chapel once or twice a week, taking 20 minutes out of my morning to recharge. The solemnity of the liturgy washed over me in a way I hadn't experienced in my nondenominational history. It was a safe and peaceful environment that soothed my soul and slowly rebuilt my confidence.

It was the right ring at the right time.

I spent nearly two years at the university. I helped grow the adult degree programs similar to the one I'd taken to get my bachelor's degree. I became a mentor to younger colleagues. I toyed with the idea of getting a PhD. I rebuilt the skills I needed to get back in the ring.

If you're freshly wounded, take your time. Don't rush straight to the main stage black belt division. Yes—get in the ring. But find the right ring for this time in your life. I spent 21 months in a job that allowed me to ease back into the fight. Challenge yourself, but don't set yourself up for failure and discouragement. Just like martial artists progress from belt rank to belt rank, you'll find yourself moving up into more challenging divisions as you gain strength, agility, confidence, and courage. It's not important that you get there today—it's important that you're in the arena, finding the right ring for the right time.

Take some time to honestly assess your own circumstances and to find your right ring.

Cindy at Lone Star Open

ASK YOURSELF

Where am I pouring my energy and being defeated and depleted?

_____

_____

Am I in a ring outside my division? Why am I here?

_____

_____

What keeps me in the wrong ring?

_____

_____

How can I know which is the right ring for me?

_____

_____

Once you've figured out which division to enter, but before you set foot in the ring, there's another essential step.

———

GET PREPARED

I love to see new Little Dragons. These are the four- to seven-year-olds and they are precious. Some come to their first class clinging to parents, peeking around Mom's leg or Dad's shoulder. Just getting them on the mat can be a challenge. I have one instructor who specializes in the little ones. She enters at the corner of the mat, just sitting quietly with a new, nervous Dragon. She points out what the other students are doing, asks questions about the student's favorite color or cartoon character. She's warm and loving and it's the rare child who doesn't come to trust her enough to take her hand and join the class—even if it's for the last five minutes of game time. Other Little Dragons are so eager, they run onto the mat and have to be gently told to come back off and bow politely as they enter the training area. The first few weeks are all about learning martial arts etiquette: Bowing onto our floor in a sign of respect for the learning space. Saying, "Yes, ma'am!" when the instructors speaks. Bowing a polite greeting to the students on the mat. Martial arts, as I tell the new parents, is far more than kicking and punching. It's a way of life, even for our tiniest students.

It's especially delightful to see them lead warmups. We start with our senior Dragons and each one performs an exercise. Five-year-old brown belt Jeremy, his dimples deeper than any I've ever seen, runs to the front of the class. "Jumping jacks on my count, yes, sir?" The class responds with a hearty "Yes, sir!" and they begin. Arms and legs flying everywhere, they just love to hop about. After twenty of something that somewhat resembles a jumping jack, Jeremy runs back into line, replaced by six-year-old blue belt Theresa. "Cherry pickers on my account, yes, ma'am?" Her wild mane of curls refuses to be held by a measly hair tie and springs out as she bends and counts, "One, two, three...." The instructors all grin at each other hearing the "on my account." Little Dragons are known for their malapropisms and we never correct them. It's one of the most enchanting things about teaching them.

It's delightful to see newly minted purple belt Little Dragons. These are the intermediate students who are ready to start sparring, although their parents aren't always quite ready. The students are excited to move into the intermediate belt rank but, most important, they are excited to get in the ring and test their skills. At my studio, we don't let students start sparring until they've reached a stage where they are proficient in some techniques. They begin learning the eight-block system as white belts, adding the counter punches at gold belt, the end of their beginner rank. By purple belt, they are ready to test what they've learned in the ring.

Little Dragons also get very excited about acquiring their sparring gear. Some want all black; others want all pink. Some like a kaleidoscope of items: blue headgear, red footgear, white handgear. I've had parents tell me their kiddos actually wore their sparring gear to bed, they were so excited to receive it. There may be nothing more adorable than a Little Dragon all padded up in brand new gear. They look a bit like the Pillsbury Doughboy!

Oddly enough, when the time comes to step into the ring, lots of my students want to skip the time-consuming task of gearing up. I'll see parents trying to get them to stop squirming as they strap on each piece. The tiny but mighty fighters get their gloves and headgear on and want to rush right out into the ring, they are so eager to get to it. They get frustrated when we insist on them donning every piece of protection. What seemed so wonderful when it arrived is now an annoyance.

Before they get to spar another student one on one, they have to work on sparring drills while wearing their gear. That also can frustrate them. Why repeat a drill over and over when you could skip them and just get out there and fight? They assume that because they have their own gear, they're ready for the match. Drills can be tedious, yes. But practicing and becoming proficient at specific techniques in response to an opponent's moves means that my students are able to react quickly and successfully—which is what I want if they ever have to actually use the stuff! We run them through scenarios: How should I react to a back fist to my temple? Upper defense, reverse punch. Or defensive side kick. Or bob and weave, uppercut. There are lots of options...if they actually remember what to do. Repetitive drills give my little students the opportunity to build the skills they can rely on without even thinking.

Even black belts need protective gear and lots of practice. Preparing for a tournament or a belt test (especially a Mastery test) requires full gear and months or years of training. Now there is no game time at the end of class. And while they enjoy sparring their classmates, they are very serious about learning—and winning. I rotate my black belts through sparring drills, with first degrees sparring fourth degrees at some point in the class. Each of them knows to moderate power and speed based on the match up. And when two fourth degree men are paired up, it's hard to pay attention to everyone else, as their skill and passion are beautiful to watch. My favorite moment, however, is when the sweet-tempered Little Dragons teacher head kicks one of the fourth-degree men. It's her sneaky approach—a fake front kick that turns into a high round kick—that routinely surprises opponents. Everyone in class knows to watch out for it but everyone succumbs at some point.

We train hard, knowing the Mastery test will be difficult, but not as difficult as a true self-defense experience. We have to be ready for both, and it takes a deep commitment to preparation and training. As I prepare my students, it's inconceivable for me to spend a paltry amount of time or effort on such a momentous trial. Without adequate preparation, not only will they fail their test, they're apt to get injured. Getting prepared for the testing ring is lengthy and sometimes laborious.

But preparation is essential. It's more than getting ready for a sparring match: It's a fantastic metaphor, one we need before reentering the ring of life.

Taking time to prepare may seem burdensome to a Little Dragon. But the lesson is one I hope they'll remember for life, not just for martial arts. In the same way, I've learned the hard way not to enter situations either professionally and personally where I'm unprotected and unprepared.

Far too often we make emotional decisions instead of critically thinking through the implications and taking smart risks. We've gotten past the fear and concern of getting back in the ring and we've done the hard work to determine which ring is ours. But then we decide to just go for it, acting like one of my Little Dragons, diving in without doing the necessary work to prepare. If I don't prepare my students through rigorous training and providing the appropriate protective gear, I am dooming them to fail.

Knowing I'm prepared—mentally, physically, emotionally, and spiritually—allows me to take wise risks and achieve things I'd never imagined.

Consider what you need. If your preparation need is professional, what does that look like? After my first divorce, I knew I needed to go back to school. Living in Silicon Valley, there was no way I would be able to provide for my sons as a single mother without a degree. It was obvious what I needed—but not necessarily how I could get it. After lots of research, I found a two-year degree completion program where I could go to class one night per week. It met my needs, although I had to take out loans and make lots of sacrifices to get it done. By committing to the rigors of a bachelor's degree program, I gradually prepared to take on more and more challenging professional roles. Every level of preparation gave me greater confidence, skill, and experience—and awakened me to better opportunities. Some days were tedious, like sparring drills. But they were necessary to launch me into the ring.

Maybe your need for preparation is different. Maybe it's not education—instead, you need to prepare your mind and heart. You've come to the place where you're ready to get back into the fight and you've determined which ring to enter. But you have baggage—old equipment that needs to be replaced. It could be anxiety that is holding you back or perfectionism. Do you need to sign up for a yoga class, a painting class, or an improv program? It could be that you need to learn how to relax and quiet your spirit. I started doing hot yoga years ago as a complement to my martial arts training. The beauty of the moves and their drawn-out expression was completely opposite the punctuated nature of my martial arts techniques. The heat and the culture forced me to slow down, to be vastly more mindful, to stop competing with myself. It was the additional preparation I needed for facing hardship in a way I had not learned through martial arts.

Or maybe you're just really tightly wound and you need to let out your inner diva. Letting go terrifies you! I have a friend, an amazing entrepreneur who opened a pole dancing studio in Austin. She specializes in working with women who need to defeat insecurity—not learn how to be strippers. Even the least athletic women learn incredible skills after training with her. The physical and emotional strength her students gain from their training makes them formidable women, bursting with power and confidence, ready to jump into the ring.

So who knows? Maybe you need some six-inch stilettos and a pole. Opening our minds to new approaches—*refusing to perceive things the way we always have*—is part of getting prepared.

Whatever your preparation needs are, now is not the

time to gut it out, sticking to what you've done in the past. Invest in yourself and get the training and preparation you need to take on the world...and step into your stronger, more powerful future.

In 2010, I found out about my second husband's infidelity with one of our adult martial arts students. I had been pretty certain it was happening, yet when he told me, it still felt like a sick gut punch. One night we'd been watching a movie and when it was over, I started to get up to go to bed. He stopped me by starting to talk about something stupid—something to just put me in a defensive mood. Then he said, "So I've been unfaithful to you. You need to know that." Just like that.

I asked with whom and for how long. He told me the woman's name, confirming my suspicions. He said it was over, but it had gone on for six months. The woman had brazenly come to visit me in the hospital a few months earlier when I had my knee replaced. I had always felt negatively toward her but thought it was just me. I actually tried very hard to be kind to her, spending extra time after classes to work with her. She came to my cardio-kickboxing classes and I complimented her on her weight loss. I kept having a strong feeling around her—almost revulsion—and redoubled my efforts to be nice and not let it show. She was fawning over my 25-year-old son, an instructor at the studio, which further bothered me. I trusted him to see it for what it was, but it annoyed me nonetheless. So learning it was her wasn't a surprise, just a reason to mentally slap myself for not listening to my intuition.

I felt a dull nausea and then a cold hardness. I walked downstairs to our bedroom, packed an overnight bag and my laptop, and got in my car. It was midnight and I had no idea where I was going—I just knew I had to get out of my house. I drove south for a couple of hours and finally stopped at 3:00 a.m., randomly choosing a hotel on the side of the highway. After a couple of hours of deeply troubled sleep, I went downstairs for a cup of coffee and a bagel. Back in my room, I tried to decide what was next. It suddenly became obvious to me where I needed to go: the beach. There was nowhere more essential for my soul.

I got back on the road. Ignoring his phone calls, I drove down to the Gulf, stopped at Target for a bikini, towel, and sunscreen. I stopped for a latte and spent the day baking in the sun, reading a book. Refusing to think. But it wasn't going to be enough—I had to go home at some point. I arrived late that night.

We'd been going to marriage counseling for a few months, but a couple of days later, I started individual counseling. I was completely unprepared for how to handle the disaster of my marriage and my life, and therapy was the start of me reasserting control—of dusting off and putting on my gear. After a few sessions, my therapist told me about a group he was starting. It would be six women who would meet with him weekly for 12 weeks. He wanted me to join.

I was horrified.

"The last thing in the world I want is to sit around with a bunch of women and talk about our cheating husbands," I groused. "And you know I can't stand most women anyway." My therapist smiled indulgently at me, well acquainted with my history of challenging female relationships. "Trust me," he said. "This isn't a group of victims. Every one of these women is strong—just like you. And the whole point of the group is to reclaim your identity—not just to bitch." He took a moment to fix me with a serious, caring look, and then delivered the (gut)punch line: "I'd like you to prayerfully consider it."

Now he was teaming up with God to get me into this group. With a bunch of women? Ugh.

But I trusted him and I did pray...and I decided to give it a try. I called to tell him I'd be there that week. "But if I don't like it after a week, I'm not coming back," I warned. All my walls were up and I was prepared to dislike every woman in the group.

Ten years later, we still meet every other Tuesday night. The single tattoo on my body is a tribute to our sisterhood.

That group was exactly what I needed and continues to be the ongoing preparation I need for life. The most profound lesson I learned was that preparation can take on many faces and, in the midst of tragedy, we need to be open to how it manifests. It may not be what you expected or thought you needed. I never in a million years thought I could need a group of women by my side, but I have gained a powerful sisterhood that has sustained me through the crazy ups and downs of life for a decade. We've been through divorces, marriages, babies, surgeries, layoffs, professional successes, you name it. I am incredibly grateful to my therapist who knew me well enough to gently push me to stretch...to try something new...and to prepare for life in a new and beautiful way.

It's said that the reason Steve Jobs was always so utterly in command on stage wasn't that he was a naturally gifted presenter. It was that he rehearsed—over and over and over until he had every word, every pause, every gesture, and every facial expression memorized. It only looked fantastically relaxed and polished because he worked diligently to prepare. I'm no Steve Jobs, but I am a preparation maniac when I'm speaking in public. I am scrupulous about my appearance, trying on a variety of outfits and jewelry to ensure I can move around and feel wonderful. I try on any number of shoes to ensure they are high enough to make me feel fierce and comfortable enough to walk around the stage. And I practice. And practice. And practice. Not one tilt of the head or seconds of silence escape my scrutiny. Preparation is my superpower—in the professional world.

At the moment when my legs were kicked out from under me by my ex, I was unprepared. I thought I could do life on my own, secure in my strength and my character. It was only when I was knocked out that I realized I was wanting, that my gear wasn't on. It wasn't even in the bag. I had sabotaged my own success by seeing my marital problems as something to hide, something shameful that made me seem weak and foolish for marrying yet another wrong man. I stuck with the responses I'd always used: Tough it out. Stiff upper lip. Concentrate on working harder and not letting anyone in. I worried about the parents at my studio. What would they think? Would they leave en masse? My three older kids hated my husband. But what about my bonus son Tristan, the one I'd inherited with this marriage when he was only four, the one I'd raised? If we separated, he'd leave with his father—could I maintain a relationship with him? My sense of failure grew, but I refused to let it consume me. It was enough. I kicked my husband out.

Finally, I began to prepare to face the rest of my life—to reenter the ring.

As you stand at the entrance to your ring, there are no guarantees. I can't promise that you won't get knocked out your first time in there. But I can promise that if you fail to prepare, you really do prepare to fail. It's a hackneyed state-ment—but it's true. Prepare for what you know you will need and be willing to augment or change that training as your needs change. Do the hard prep work up front so you can reap the rewards of re-engaging *with life*. Don't limit your preparation to the obvious ideas, like classes or certifi-cations. Open your mind and your heart. Don't limit your-self to what you've done before. It may seem silly, but when

I am about to embark on something new and maybe a bit frightening, I will do what I need to do in terms of research and rehearsal and...I *always* buy a new lipstick. It's part of my preparation, making me feel confident and powerful.

Stilettos, lipstick, or a bachelor's degree? Perhaps. Maybe it's a long-term relationship with a support group.

Or maybe you just need to throw the bastard out.

Cindy Training at Her Studio

ASK YOURSELF

Where am I skimping on doing the hard work of preparation?

_____

_____

What should I be doing to train my mind, body, and spirit?

_____

_____

Whatever you need, make appropriate preparation a priority.

Make it your superpower.

———

GET COMFORTABLE WITH PUNCHES

Not long after I opened my school, two sisters started taking classes. One was in the Little Dragons program, the other in the Juniors program. Neither had ever done martial arts, but they both loved it. They progressed rapidly and, once they reached the intermediate rank, they were ready to start sparring.

When it was time for them to purchase their gear, both girls wanted all pink. Their dad asked to speak to me, concern written all over his face.

"How do you keep them safe?" he asked worriedly. "Could they get hit in the face?"

"Sure," I said. "But we only spar in class very carefully and only when they are completely padded up. There are two black belt instructors overseeing every match, and we do not let students fight to hurt each other. We're all on the same team," I assured him.

He was very concerned and not at all happy about letting his girls spar. But they were keen to start, and he came to every sparring class to watch.

One fascinating thing I've learned about girls sparring (other than that their dads usually freak out) is not that they can't handle getting hit. *It's that they don't like to hit back.*

Instead of kiyaps—the *ay-ah* a martial artist shouts when striking—I heard, "I'm sorry."

What?

I began to notice it with all my girls. They'd take a punch just fine; the boys were just as likely as the girls to cry if they got hit too hard. But the girls were uniformly apologetic. After a few weeks, I'd had enough. It was time to educate them and put a stop to the habit. I began by telling them "I'm sorry" wasn't allowed on the mat. If they were concerned, they could call time and simply ask, "Are you OK?" I gave them a couple of weeks to practice this new approach and then I started making them do pushups every time they apologized for hitting an opponent. Think about it: Do I really want my girls getting in the habit of apologizing for hitting? What happens when they actually have to defend themselves from an attack off the mat? Feeling guilty in that situation could have catastrophic consequences. I was implacable. No more "I'm sorry" on the mat.

Since then, I regularly get in trouble with the senior

black belts at our semi-annual Association black belt tests. "Your girls are hitting too hard!" they tell me. I have to try very hard not to smile and say, "Thank you." The Austin girls and women have a reputation for toughness. At one test a few years ago, one of my teenagers was testing for her second-degree belt. Part of the test includes several two-minute sparring rounds with others in the same division. Everyone is fully padded, along with face shields on their headgear. There are at least two senior black belts over-seeing each match. My student was fighting beautifully and was feeling strong and having a great time. She got matched up with a girl from one of the California schools and, even though she was tired from fighting several rounds, she began scoring over and over. The other girl, also tired, kept drop-ping her hands, and my fighter tagged her in the face and head more than once. The other girl started crying and one of the school owners working in our ring stopped the match. He sternly told my fighter not to hit to the head (which is silly, because it's legal in the national martial arts tournament rules). I took my student aside and told her not to hit to the head for the rest of the match—but to feel free to kick that high. I then told the other girl to remember that she was testing for her second-degree black belt and if she didn't want to get hit, she needed to keep her hands up!

My fighter won the match.

When we get back into the ring after suffering tragedy or loss, we already know how to take a punch. It's not pleasant and no one ever really gets used to getting hit. But we're still breathing, still moving through life, however brokenly. We may get tired and drop our hands, but we have learned that we can survive even the most hellish experiences.

But fighting back is hard. First, we aren't socialized as girls to fight. It's a generalization, yes, but how many of us grew up physically fighting? Even those of us with brothers didn't typically fist fight. My female martial arts students have to learn to purposely, deliberately, intentionally strike another person to score points.

That's hard.

And it's hard for us to do the same thing in life. What does fighting back in life look like? It's not strapping on gloves and going toe to toe with an opponent. We have to set goals and push to achieve them, goals that perhaps don't align with the people we've been trying to please. We might have to set new boundaries with people who haven't honored them. We might have to cut off relationships, change jobs, sacrifice financially, or any number of other things we don't want to do.

In 2011, I'd been separated from my second husband for ten months. I had every reason to divorce him: Even as a Christian, I had ample cause. God's not a fan of adultery. I didn't need to stay married. Unlike so many women who are trapped into marriages for financial reasons, I was (and had always been) the breadwinner. I was perfectly capable of doing life on my own. But I didn't feel right about it. I prayed. We went to counseling. I talked with my women's counseling group and my therapist. But I just didn't feel good about divorcing him. My constant refrain was that I had to be true to myself—to be a woman of integrity, no matter what. And so after ten months of separation and hours of counseling, we reconciled.

Looking back, I cannot say what good came of the reconciliation other than further cementing my relationship to Tristan. He had called me Mom since he was six years old. His own mother was out of the picture and I was able to be the parent Tristan needed. Was that worth five more years of problems? I look at him now, and I can't say it wasn't. In 2020 when his father completely unraveled, I was there to pick up the pieces of my son's life.

Despite my efforts, after five years we were done. And once I got over the shock of him being the one to bail out of the marriage, I was thoroughly convinced it was the right thing. But that didn't mean it was easy.

I'm a "nice girl." I've always been a nice girl, never wanting to cause anyone problems, always willing to take a punch—even when someone else deserved it. After the 2016 Mastery test, I got back to Austin, determined to take control of my school and my life. Taking the job at the university, with such a huge cut in salary, was a gut punch. But I took it because I needed steady income and health benefits.

I dug into the finances at my martial arts school and added experienced board members who could help. I had been writing personal checks to make payroll and pay operational expenses for months. I drained my savings account, took out money from my 401k. These were more punches to the face, but I took them to keep my business alive.

I hired an attorney to help me hang onto my retirement funds and the house I'd purchased, spending money I couldn't afford in order to protect my assets from a predatory husband who was trying to take the half he reminded me "I'm entitled to." It was a kick to the knees that threatened to knock me off my feet, but I took it to make sure I had a future.

He won a few rounds. Multiple adulteries, near financial ruin. Peeling back the layers of our life over 12 years showed over and over where he had betrayed me, my family, our students.

And then I fought back.

Can't pay your half of the studio deficit each month? What a shame. Relinquish your shares in the corporation.

Want to take on students and train them in your garage? Nope. Violates the five mile rule the Association has for opening new schools. Start your own damn organization.

Nobody knows about your proclivity for adultery and embezzlement? Not keeping your secrets anymore. Reap what you sow.

It wasn't easy. Every single time I had to go on the offensive, it was uncomfortable. But no one wins a sparring match by being exclusively defensive. You have to score points to win a match and you have to fight back to reclaim your life.

You may be very good at taking a punch. My favorite fighters have a great chin—the ability to take a brutal punch and remain standing, able to finish the round. But we aren't professional fighters, are we? We don't get paid big bucks to go five or ten or 12 rounds. And being a punching bag—literally or figuratively—is a terrible skill. No one—absolutely no one—has the right to demean, degrade, demote, demolish, or delegitimize us.

Where do you need to punch back?

Cindy at BB Demo. Photo: Andrew Moore

ASK YOURSELF

Where am I taking a punch that legitimately should go to someone else?

_____

_____

How does it serve me to avoid letting others take responsibility for their actions?

_____

_____

What prevents me from fighting back?

_____

_____

What can I do today to stop taking punches for others?

_____

_____

Life has a full arsenal of offensive weapons and it's great to remain standing in the face of a flurry of its punches.
It's far better to fight back.

DON'T FIGHT MAD

When I was a blue belt, I loved to spar. But I got incredibly frustrated if someone beat me. I'd become visibly angry. When I sparred with my instructor—and lost every time— he stopped the round and scolded me: "Don't fight mad! *When you fight mad, you don't see what's coming and you miss opportunities.*"

Talk about a life lesson.

The absolute worst decisions we make are frequently made in the heat of negative emotions—*reactions* rather than responses. When I was angry at losing, I'd tighten up and throw techniques without thought, hoping power would substitute for strategy. It never worked. Invariably, I'd leave myself open to counterattacks that scored and further frustrated me.

However, anger isn't the only emotion that clouds our judgment. There's resentment. Bitterness. Lack of forgiveness. Regret. Jealousy. All these negative emotions can dull our ability to genuinely see and take advantage of wonderful opportunities. They hide beauty and rob us of healing and peace.

We don't see what's coming and we miss opportunities.

Cindy at 5th Degree Mastery Test

FIGHTING MAD: JOSH'S STORY

Josh was a mess. "I just wanted to fit in," he told me. "I was a rebel without a cause."

Josh grew up the eldest of three children in a stable, two-parent, middle class family. They are devout Christians, and Josh attended church and youth group regularly as a child. Josh was an exceptional athlete, a talented pitcher like his father, who'd played and coached professional baseball. But in his late teens, Josh started smoking weed and then moved to stronger drugs. In his twenties, he went off the rails. "From drugs," he told me, "I went to guns." After a few years of running wild, he found himself in prison for a year. His family was frantic. How could this have happened to their son?

The first Sunday after his release from prison, his parents picked him up to take him to church. "I was all in my Scarface gear," he told me ruefully. Nothing had changed. Josh was still a bitter young man and he went right back to the same life, feeling resentful rather than repentant. But this time, he noticed that his old friends weren't going anywhere in life. It troubled him, and he slowly began making small changes, separating from bad influences. He got a construction job at a major company owned by one of the church elders. In spite of his wild past, Josh was an excellent worker and began to build a reputation for diligence and excellence. But he continued to abuse alcohol, ending up with a DUI that lost him the job where he'd been making good money and building a career.

"I was so selfish," he told me. "I didn't care about anyone." All of his decisions stemmed from anger, resentment, and bitterness. He made choices from negative emotions rather than hope or happiness and refused to look at the role his emotions played in the life he now experienced. He'd visit his family and it became an occasion for chaos rather than family bonding. "I saw everyone making money, having a life. I wanted that, too." But all he created was broken relationships, financial hardships, a prison record, and anger.

THE AWAKENING

Josh got a job working with his father at an elite baseball club in San José, at 50% of his construction salary. He watched his dad coaching and, for the first time, he truly *saw* his father. Josh saw how happy his dad was, doing what he loved. "I started noticing the little kids' smiles when they hit the ball for the very first time, not off the tee," he mused. At the same time, he watched one of his mother's best friends—a woman virtually his own age—struggling with cancer. "Seeing what she goes through, I have nothing to worry about," he realized. Something began to change in his heart. It was time to let the anger go.

It was time to stop fighting mad.

And then his family moved from California to Texas. Now there was no fallback, no place to crash if things went wrong, if he failed again.

Josh had a friend who worked as a contractor at a big Silicon Valley corporation. His friend got him a job—and Josh determined that this time, things would be different. He didn't want to let his friend down, and he worked hard to prove his value to the company. Without a high school diploma, Josh didn't have the requisite credentials, yet he was a hard worker, tenacious and intelligent. And he had a newfound passion for learning and for fighting in a positive way.

———

As my instructor told me, "Fighting mad" means not seeing what's coming and missing opportunities. Fighting mad is so much more than living with anger. When we are consumed with bitterness and regret, it's far too easy to simply repeat unhealthy behaviors that perpetuate our sense of failure and can ruin relationships that could otherwise nurture our growth. When we begin to release the chains that bind and rot our emotions—that devastate our souls—only then are we open to finding the right ring, the healthy environment where we can plant ourselves and truly flourish. Letting go isn't an overnight, one-and-done effort. It takes time, patience, and a refusal to continue drowning in negative emotions and memories. It takes work and courage—it takes a commitment to fight.

And it takes acknowledging that you deserve more.

————

Within four years, Josh became the go-to troubleshooter for his company, traveling all over the world to improve logistics at various facilities. A high school dropout, Josh has received numerous accolades from executive management for his thorough, no nonsense approach to operational excellence. His misplaced rebellion and selfishness are now transformed. As he told me, "It took a while, but it's all about the team now. I don't care about personal achievement—I want my team to succeed." He's left a trail of success across the United States, the United Kingdom, and Brazil, among other locations.

Things have happened to all of us that made us feel *less than*. We've absorbed abuse—physical, verbal, emotional, financial, spiritual—and we've found ways to blame ourselves. In other cases, we made really poor decisions that left us feeling ashamed, stupid, or guilty. No matter the cause of our pain, we all deserve to move forward in freedom. To climb the steps into our ring fully prepared and emboldened to fight our fight, theme song blaring around us. In order to release the negative emotions that hold us down and drive us to fight mad, we have to believe that we deserve a better life, that *we have what it takes* to create a better life, and that *it's possible* to secure a better life. No fighter walks into a ring expecting or planning to lose.

In April 1983, I got married for the first time. It was a foolish thing to do, but I jumped in and committed to making it work. I got pregnant right away—not planned, but not unwanted. In fact, it couldn't have been more different from when I got pregnant as a teenager. The second time, I was 21 and a grown woman (at least in my own mind), I was married, I knew what to expect. I decided that in every respect, this pregnancy and birth would be completely different from the first. Memories of being a scared, physically and emotionally abused, teenaged mom were jammed and crammed...I wanted nothing to do with them. I hadn't dealt with the pain but I was sure as hell not going to repeat it.

In 1984, it wasn't automatic that a woman could expect to have a vaginal delivery after having a previous Caesarean section. My doctor—the very obstetrician who'd delivered my brother and me—was progressive. He told me that it was my decision, and I made it clear I wanted this birth to be a complete 180 degrees from the last one. No C-section for me. We went to all the birthing classes and prepared for a traditional delivery.

The pregnancy progressed and all was well. A week before the baby was due, my doctor reminded me that the method of delivery was my decision, and that if I changed my mind and wanted a C-section, we needed to schedule it. He reiterated the risks, as well as his commitment to my decision. I scoffed—no C-section for me. I was Team Natural all the way.

I knew the risks. But as a Christian woman, I was utterly certain that God would never allow anything to happen to my baby. I didn't share that with my doctor, but I was positive I was on strong theological ground. God wasn't going to hurt my baby. No way.

Two days later, I was struck with the inescapable feeling that I should have a C-section.

It was so strong, so powerful—I couldn't get away from it. But I tried. I fought. I prayed and challenged God, "Why would you ask me to do this? I'm not going to. This time it's different! I'm married. I'm a grown up. I have another child to care for. You cannot ask me to do this. *I refuse*." My fury was palpable. I all but stomped my feet in immature rage.

I talked to my husband. What did he think? No use. "If God's talking to you; it's your decision." Thanks for nothing.

The next morning, I was reading my Bible, continuing to argue with God, reminding him that he's supposed to be for us and on the side of goodness and love. And as I read, I came across the story of Jesus being tempted by the devil:

"Then the devil took him into the holy city and had him stand on the pinnacle of the temple, and said to him, 'If you are the Son of God, throw yourself down; for it is written, "He will command his angels concerning you" and "On their hands they will bear you up, so that you will not strike your foot against a stone."'

Jesus said to him, 'On the other hand, it is written,' "You shall not put the Lord your God to the test."'

— *MATTHEW* 4:5-7

It wasn't an unfamiliar story. I'd read it hundreds of times, but now I saw myself on the pinnacle of the temple, prepared to throw my baby off because I was sure God was somehow constrained to give me what I wanted. Like a slap in the face, I realized I was making my decision out of fear. Out of regret. Out of hurt that had never healed. I wasn't deciding from a place of wisdom and peace—I was fighting mad.

I called the doctor and scheduled the surgery for that Friday.

The day arrived and we got to the hospital. While I had been wide awake during my daughter's birth, for this one, I had to be knocked out—for some reason, the epidural only took on one side of my body. As the surgeon began, I shouted, "*I can feel that!*" The anesthesiologist leaned over and calmly told me, "We're going to have to put you out." I don't remember another word.

While I was completely out, I hallucinated wildly. I found myself on a looping, seemingly endless slide that was half yellow and half bright pink, with big black arrows showing me which direction to go. Not that I needed them. I raced along the slide, doing 360-degree loops, nearly flying along. And throughout the entire crazy ride, all I could think was, "I have to go faster. I have to get to the hospital to meet my baby!" I had wanted a completely different experience, but this wasn't at all what I'd fought God for.

Finally, the anesthesiologist brought me back to consciousness. Still in the throes of the drugs, my first words were, "Did they get the baby? Did they forget to get the baby?" My husband assured me they had gotten the baby...a boy. "What's his name?" I asked, forgetting in my haze that we'd already planned to call a boy baby James William. I lay back, spent but relieved. Jaimie, as we'd call him, was perfect.

In the recovery room, my obstetrician visited me. He was very serious as he took my hand. "Cindy, you need to thank God for the decision to have the C-section." I hadn't mentioned a word about my weeklong battle with the Almighty and we'd never had a faith conversation in the 22 years I'd known him.

"When I got through the abdominal wall, I could see the baby through your uterus—it was as thin as onion skin. The cord was wrapped twice around his neck." He took a breath. "If you'd gone into hard labor, you'd likely have lost your baby and your uterus."

———

It's easy to make really bad decisions when we are angry. Likewise, we don't see what's coming and we miss opportunities when we're frightened, resentful, bitter, or filled with regret. It's far too easy to simply admonish ourselves to "let it go," as if that weren't something we'd already attempted over and over again. And yet, to move on—to truly have a fighting chance at joy—we must.

It can be seductively easy to stay in the depths of pain. When we've been victimized, traumatized, and hurt, it's only right that we feel deep emotion. And...it's only right that we take the steps necessary to free ourselves from the bondage of that pain. It goes back to getting prepared to enter the ring: What do I need in order to liberate myself from these painful chains?

Therapy has been a mainstay of my life for years and maybe that can work for you. Perhaps finding a counselor you genuinely trust and connect with is the right decision. Or it's starting martial arts and punching and kicking your way out of sadness and insecurity into power and confidence. I don't pretend to know or understand your particular situation—what it is that's left you yearning for freedom. Only you know what it is for you. I know what it is for me.

And once we name it, we can fight it. There is power in speaking the truth about what has happened to us.

My decision to insist on a natural delivery for my son nearly cost him his life. It wasn't a decision made from research and wisdom. It was born in the toxic ooze of fear and pain and insecurity and profound guilt. And the only one who could change that was me.

Emotions—even powerfully negative ones—can be beneficial. But when we allow unresolved anger, bitterness, frustration, or remorse to hinder our ability to make healthy decisions, we simply must have the courage to ask ourselves hard questions...and listen to the answers.

LEARNING TO RELEASE

When I arrived in California for my sixth-degree black belt test in 2016, I knew I would be the oldest person on my team. I made the silent commitment that I would do every single thing asked of me—no, I would do more. If someone faltered, it wouldn't be me. I'd be the one picking up the slack. There was no way I would give anyone any reason to bemoan the fact that a 50-something grandmother was a teammate. When we carried a 400-pound log through the streets of San Francisco for eight hours, I took extra turns and helped basket-carry injured teammates across the Golden Gate Bridge. When we practiced martial arts in a shadeless field for hours in 104 degree heat, I shared water and offered encouragement to my entire team. And when we shivered while doing our bo staff fighting routine on a windy beach, I never stopped pushing my body and my mind to excel.

I succeeded beyond my expectations: I was part of a winning team, getting accolades throughout the six grueling days. I had an amazing time doing what I love.

But then I came back to Austin. My soon-to-be-second-ex-husband was still my business partner. We were bleeding money at the martial arts studio; we were losing $4000 every month. I didn't want to make him angry, because he was manipulative and sabotaged any effort I made to salvage the business. I wrote personal checks to make payroll and tried to figure out how to keep the doors open. I was afraid —afraid of losing my business, my reputation, and my students.

And then I realized: *I was fighting mad.* Just as my former instructor warned me, I wasn't seeing things clearly. I was missing opportunities. The realization was hard—but essential. Enough was enough.

I asked myself the hard questions and I refused to give in to fear and uncertainty or my ex's lies. Instead, I let him know that since we were 50/50 partners in our corporation, I expected him to make up 50 percent of the deficit each month. When he refused, citing his lack of income, I told him that it was time for him to resign his shares and leave the company.

He agreed. He signed the documents divorcing himself from our business... now *my business.*

- I changed the locks.

- I changed all the passwords.
- I added people to the board of directors who were competent and strong.
- I began consulting with another school owner who'd almost lost his business but had come back from near disaster, and we put together the plans that would bring my school back from the brink.
- I emptied my savings account.
- I borrowed from my 401k.
- I put people into positions where they could excel, people who weren't afraid of the situation, who loved me and the studio.
- I rolled up my sleeves, gritted my teeth, and refused to fight mad.

Four years later, we were debt free and in the black. Our student body had increased by 30%. We made decisions based on research, logic, passion, and commitment.

I wasn't mad.
I wasn't ashamed.
I wasn't resentful.
I was successful.

And in 2020 when the coronavirus hit, I was prepared. We had money in the bank and the infrastructure to start online classes almost immediately. Making rational, fact-based, and clear-eyed decisions meant we kept our doors open and provided the services and family experience my students desperately needed, while many small businesses around the country simply couldn't survive. We were able to see things clearly and not miss opportunities. We fought smart... not mad.

Finally finding the courage to stop fighting mad meant my son lived. "Jaimie" is now James—a six-foot, five-inch brilliant young man. His strength of character, kindness, empathy, and intelligence are a gift to the universe, and one that would not exist if I'd continued fighting out of remorse and shame.

ASK YOURSELF

Where am I reacting instead of questioning?

_____

_____

Where are my risks foolish instead of intelligent?

_____

_____

Where am I allowing emotion to cloud my judgment and affect my ability to critically think through problems?

_____

_____

Where is resentment, bitterness, pain, or lack of forgiveness holding me back from joy?

_____

_____

What beautiful gifts do I forsake when I huddle behind fear? Behind anger and a lack of forgiveness?

_____

What purpose do I derail when I will not give myself the grace I deserve?

As my instructor told me so many years ago, when I fight mad, I miss opportunities and I don't see what's coming. Fight with passion, yes—but let go the destructive emotions that drive poor decisions. Live with purpose and unleash your powers for good.

MIX IT UP

When I first started martial arts, the association I joined was a tae kwon do organization. But after many years, my great grandmaster realized that tae kwon do—even though it's an awesome discipline—is insufficient in a real fight. Tae kwon do is mostly kicking, and if a fight ends up on the ground, it's not terribly effective. And so my great grandmaster started training with masters in other disciplines all over the world, broadening our curriculum so that we were proficient both standing and on the ground. We now practice elements of Muay Thai kickboxing, American boxing, Brazilian jiu-jitsu, and Filipino stick and knife fighting, in addition to our tae kwon do basics. Over my two-plus decades with the organization, we've mixed up the curriculum dramatically and it's made me a far more well-rounded martial artist.

Years ago, I had a 10-year old martial arts student. "Peter" was tall, athletic, and very eager to start sparring. Once he advanced to a belt rank high enough to put him in the ring, he couldn't wait for the next tournament. As luck would have it, the Lone Star Open was coming up—the perfect opportunity for him. In the days leading up to the competition, he attended every class. He practiced diligently, his excitement palpable. The day arrived and Peter was ready. We found the ring for the 10-year-old intermediate students and checked in with the scorekeeper. Gear on, bouncing with anticipation, he prepared to take on his first opponent. The match began, and Peter moved around the ring, bobbed and weaved...and pretty much ignored everything we had practiced before the match. His opponent scored, repeatedly. Peter became frustrated, suddenly unsure of himself. In a desperate move to avoid losing yet another point, he threw a picture-perfect cross-step axe kick that scored. "Two points, red!" shouted the referee. My student was transformed.

Suddenly, all he could do was throw axe kicks. No more punches. No more roundhouse kicks. None of the myriad techniques he'd learned in class. It was all axe kicks, all the time. We shouted from the corner, "Mix it up! Combos! Use your hands! Roundhouse kick!" Nothing penetrated his absolute conviction that axe kicks were the way to victory. And when he won his match, he was even more certain.

From then on, every sparring practice became an axe kick clinic. Even when they didn't work, he was still utterly convinced they were the key to winning and he was afraid to try anything else. I got to the point where I made him do pushups if he used an axe kick in class—it was the only way to get him to mix up his techniques.

The truth is, I've been that 10-year old. Haven't we all? We find something that works for us and we're reluctant to try anything else. It was hard enough to step out and give [fill in the blank] a try. Why would I risk trying something else?

In 2009, my career stalled. I'd been in a great job, leading a global team of over 100 people. But things went badly: the US economy was tanking and my company laid off my entire team except me and a couple of others who found roles on other teams. I was still employed, but I was floundering. No one knew what to do with me, and I worried that I was next to hit the unemployment line. It was kind of like being a tae kwon do practitioner suddenly finding herself on the ground. The same old kicks just weren't suited to the job.

Physically I was taking a beating, too. I have a congenital problem with my joints and had already had four surgeries on my right knee to mend a torn meniscus, bone spurs, and a cracked patella. By December 2009, the arthritis had progressed to the point where a replacement was pretty much my only answer. The surgery went fine, but the rehab was miserable. Because I was so young and healthy, the scar tissue grew quickly, and my flexibility was impacted. Even when my six-foot tall physical therapist pushed hard on my knee, I couldn't straighten my leg completely. I ended up taking three months off work and had to go back under anesthesia to rip apart the scar tissue that was limiting my mobility.

And in the final gut punch to the combination, that's when I found out my second husband was cheating on me with one of our adult students.

So I did what *I always did*—in my first-born, good girl, responsible version of the never-ending axe kick. I dusted off my résumé. I worked hard at my rehab. I read my Bible and I prayed. Do the right thing. Do the responsible thing. Keep smiling and meeting other people's needs.

I started job hunting, but there were very few companies that could provide a comparable salary and allow the remote work that my current job did. I kept up with all my obligations at work and the studio, never batting an eye, never sharing my pain. People didn't know my husband and I were separated. I didn't even tell my mom because she was dying of cancer and I didn't want to upset her—despite the fact that I desperately needed her help to process my pain. I didn't tell my family that my marriage—*my second marriage!*—was falling apart.

Axe kick, axe kick, axe kick.

But the same approach didn't work anymore. I was miserable and stuck in a loop of behavior that was utterly ineffective.

I had always wanted to get my MBA, but the timing never seemed quite right. Suddenly I was in a place where I had the time. It wasn't a matter of getting the degree to get a better job. It was a matter of doing something for me—something to challenge myself, something I would enjoy. Something that would rebuild my confidence and give me a win. So...*finally*...I mixed it up. I looked into a number of programs, but nothing met my needs. One was too expensive; another wasn't the right schedule. I reluctantly decided that it wasn't—again—the right time. I had resigned myself to staying in the same *sameness*...and then one day, I was driving and listening to NPR. A commercial came on for the MBA program at Concordia University, a campus that was 15 minutes from my home. It was the perfect situation for me: a two year, one night per week program focusing on leadership. I scheduled an appointment with an admissions counselor, worked like crazy to get all my application paperwork together to start with the next cohort, and got accepted. Eight weeks later, I started classes, thrilled to be back in school. I worked my high tech marketing job in the daytime, taught my martial arts classes in the evenings and weekends, and did homework until the wee hours of the morning and all day on Saturdays. I didn't sleep a lot for those two years, but I finished Sigma Beta Delta with straight As.

That degree didn't get me a new job and it put me in debt for more than a few years. But it built muscles that had atrophied or never fully developed, *muscles that were for me alone*—a concept I'd never considered. Even the classes I didn't particularly care for brought me the joy of accomplishment and a chance to do what I loved:

Learn.

By mixing things up, I learned the invaluable lesson that self-care is vital and that no one was going to do it for me. I could finally ignore the siren call of the axe kick.

When I got laid off and my second husband filed for divorce, I was fortunate to have a generous friend with a beautiful lake house. As I took the time to wander her beautiful property, sit on the dock overlooking Lake Austin, lie out on the grass, or just curl up in bed, I thought hard about what I wanted in life—personally and professionally. Those five weeks gave me the time I needed to reevaluate my choices and clear my mind.

Sitting at her kitchen table with my laptop, I started my own marketing agency, Knockout Marketing Strategies. I fought tenaciously to keep the house I'd purchased for us and the money I'd earned, despite living in a state that was determined to rob me of both. I slept and cried when I need to, took pride in the body I was building through rigorous training, and continued to prepare for my black belt test in California that summer.

About a month before going to San José, I was on the phone with my brother. He told me he'd planned a trip to Cabo San Lucas with his sons the week right after my black belt test. I was jealous—I hadn't been on vacation for quite some time. He told me, "Why don't you just join us? It's on me." Before I could get excited at the idea, axe kick girl jumped in—how could I take a second week off after the black belt test? Wasn't it irresponsible to spend the money flying to Cabo when I should fly back to Austin and get back to work building my fledgling business? I didn't have a job—did I really have the right to go on vacation?

Damn right, I did. I booked the flight.

After I finished the test and celebrated with my students, I took a rideshare at 1:00 a.m. to my brother's house in San José. I crashed for a couple of hours on his couch and then groggily awaited the ride to the airport. I slept most of the way to Cabo, my body, mind, heart, and spirit completely spent. Once we arrived at the beautiful resort my brother had booked, I did absolutely nothing I didn't want to do for an entire glorious week. And at the end of that commitment to self-care, I flew back to Austin and back to my life, renewed and reinvigorated. It was utterly different from anything I'd ever done in my life, and *it was absolutely the right thing.*

Mixing it up is rarely easy. It takes courage to do things

we've never done before. It may sound ridiculous to say choosing to spend a week at a resort in Mexico required bravery. But deciding to spend money and time on a trip solely for the purpose of self-care was revolutionary for me. For this nice little firstborn Christian girl who always tries to do the responsible thing, takes care of everyone else, and always puts herself last, it took more than a little courage. And it kicked me into a new way of living and thinking about life: I realized that part of the fight to reclaim my joy must include doing things differently. *I had to mix it up, because the old techniques no longer served me*—if they ever had.

The next year was a complete mosaic of good and bad. But I refused to go backward. I continued to mix it up.

WHAT IF?

My son-in-law got a job in Florida and my daughter and her family left Texas, moving to New Smyrna Beach, a quaint village on the Atlantic coast. My daughter invited me to visit and assured me I would love it—she compared her new residence to my favorite beach back home in California. I went out to spend a week with my family and she was right: It reminded me of Capitola, the village where I'd spent so much time as a teen and young adult, the beach I took my children to for years. Everything within walking distance. Adorable shops and restaurants. The nostalgia was lovely, and as I walked on the Florida beach I wondered, *Was I ready to mix it up again?*

I had responsibilities. My martial arts studio needed me —I was the master instructor and the owner. I had gotten a job at the university that required me to be in Austin, working on campus and meeting business partners in person. I owned a beautiful home. Could I even consider leaving Austin? Axe kick girl reminded me that we don't always get what we want and that I should just stick with what I had. But the huge pay cut I'd taken meant I had to take a loan out against my 401k just to pay my monthly bills. My son James had stayed with me for a couple of months before leaving for England—otherwise, the five-bedroom house was empty.

I started just peeking at real estate in New Smyrna Beach. Shockingly, a two-bedroom house on the Atlantic coast was far less than my home in Austin. I began to argue with myself. *What if?* I asked. *Yes, but,* I responded.

Yes, but WHAT IF?

Without a job in Florida and needing to be in Austin, I began concocting a crazy idea, mixing it up wildly: *What if* I split my time between both places? I talked to Rebecca for her insight. I talked to a real estate agent. I talked to my therapist. I prayed. And then I sat down with my son Alex.

Alex was a licensed massage therapist in Austin but had moved back to California to work in the cannabis industry for a couple of years. Somewhat disenchanted by the people he'd worked with, he was considering a move back to Texas to resume his career. "What if," I asked him, "you got your license in Florida? I'd buy a house and you'd live there to take care of the property and the pets. You'd pick me up at the airport once or twice a month and I'd come out for long weekends." I was convinced it was the perfect plan. As for Alex? Not so much.

Uh, no thanks. I don't want to live with my mom.

I explained that this wasn't moving back in with his mother. This was property management—and I'd pay the bills as his salary. He agreed to go to Florida with me to check out the area and then make his decision. Like me, he loved the little village, the proximity to the beach, and the fresh start. He agreed to my proposal. We left Florida and I went back to Austin, Alex to California to wrap up his life there. Over the next few months, I sold my five-bedroom house and bought a tiny two-bedroom cottage, minutes away from my daughter and her family and a whopping two-and-a-half minute walk from the beach. We packed all my things into a moving van and the boys drove it out to Florida while I followed by plane. I signed the closing documents, had a new air conditioner installed—the AC decided to die the day I finalized the purchase—and moved in.

But what about when I had to be in Austin?

Talk about mixing it up.

My best friend and her family live in Austin. They followed me out to Texas and just happen to have a couple of spare bedrooms. When I'm in Austin, I am essentially homeless, so my dearest friend gifted me with a bedroom. They take me to the airport when it's time to go home to Florida. They don't mind me coming and going at odd hours with my odd schedule, and they let me park my car in the garage. And when my second ex-husband went completely off the rails, they let my son Tristan move in, too. As my best friend says, "It's family." But it's not at all the situation any of us imagined. At nearly sixty, I live in someone's spare bedroom like some impoverished college student. Nevertheless, getting back in the fight meant reconsidering everything about my life. It meant reevaluating the things I'd always done and saying yes to new and seemingly crazy things.

I now have an excellent head instructor at my school. I have a brilliant board of directors. Tristan is a third-degree black belt and one of my top instructors. I'm able to be gone far more than a couple of long weekends each month. With this new freedom, I spend months at a time in Florida. I continue to mix it up every chance I get, learning and growing and committing to self-care and new adventures. There have been ups and downs, for sure—the air conditioner was only the first of many challenges. Hurricanes, anyone? And then that time I found out that my house (built on sand in 1958) was sinking and needed $12,000 of steel posts to level it out? And then the Christmas when the roof leaked and my dining room ceiling fell apart and we had to have Christmas dinner in the living room? It's not perfect and it's not always easy being semi-nomadic. But it's home.

ACCEPT REALITY... AND IMPROVE IT

When my mom died, it was only three weeks before she and my dad would have celebrated their 51st wedding anniversary. Their marriage was far from perfect, but they stayed together in spite of their differences and they loved each other deeply. I assumed that's how life was going to be: I'd be married until one of us was dead. We'd grow old together and go for walks around the block holding hands. But that's not how my life turned out.

I could scream about it. I could shake my fist at God. I could be miserable and muddle through the rest of my life bemoaning the fact that I'm not a senator or a wife or whatever else I might have wanted at one time. I could just continue to do the same thing forever, getting the same lousy results.

Or I could mix it up.

If you've been afraid to try something new, open your mind and heart to something small. You don't have to move four states away—switch your lipstick color to start! I'm truly not being facetious; honor what you can manage today *but don't stop there.* As the old adage says, "If you always do what you've always done, you'll always get what you've always got." Where you are on your healing journey will determine how much you're willing to push yourself. Remember, though, that every step forward is blessed progress. This isn't about being reckless—*it's about taking care of you*, your feelings, your confidence, your identity.

New Smyrna Beach, Florida

ASK YOURSELF

Where am I doing the same thing over and over?

_____

_____

Where are my techniques not leading to the success I long for?

_____

_____

What changes am I willing to make? How big am I willing to go?

_____

_____

What am I afraid of?

_____

_____

What outcomes can I imagine if I were to mix things up today?

_____

_____

Sticking with the same old techniques may produce some success, but mixing things up can bring you opportunities you never knew existed.
Like life on the beach.

———

LISTEN TO YOUR COACH

"Danielle" walked up to me one night after cardio kickboxing class—a student in her mid-thirties, in absolutely perfect shape. A long-distance runner, she had started taking my cardio classes to cross-train. She'd done so well, she'd even started teaching at my school, building a devoted community of women who loved her hard 6:00 a.m. workouts and vibrant energy.

But tonight, she was fighting back tears.

"Could I talk to you for a minute?" she asked. We stepped aside and she asked me, hesitantly, "Do you think I could do martial arts? I haven't even mentioned this to my husband. Does that sound stupid? Do you think I could do it?"

I was delighted—I hadn't started martial arts until I was

in my thirties and I knew she could not only "do martial arts," she'd be outstanding at it. I love it when adult women take the plunge and start martial arts training. I get a great deal of satisfaction at watching them gain confidence, strength, and sculpt their bodies. I was moved by her trepidation and embarrassment, though. It was a lesson for me that even a woman who appeared to be completely put together could have insecurities and fears, and that how I responded to her would have a powerful effect. I told her without hesitation that she could be a martial artist and that I would be proud to teach her and one day strap a black belt around her waist.

And so her journey started. Danielle threw herself into her training, coming to class regularly and celebrating every single milestone. When she passed her white belt test and moved up to orange belt, she threw a party. The house was decked out in orange; all the food was orange. When she picked up her orange balloons at the store, she informed the clerk that she was throwing herself a party to celebrate earning her orange belt. When the clerk asked, "So that's almost black belt, right?" she responded, "Yes! It's almost black belt." The fact that black belt was three years away became our running joke.

Over the next three years, there were plenty of times Danielle struggled. Turns out running hundreds of miles a year doesn't necessarily translate into great martial arts skills. And while she was an excellent athlete, she still needed regular pep talks from me to inspire and build her confidence. For one tournament, she practiced and practiced, preparing herself for the adult women's division sparring matches. Once in the ring, however, she just blanked. One of my black belts and I stood on the sidelines, shouting encouragement. Between rounds, we reminded her of the techniques she should use. We shouted and shouted—to no avail.

Danielle needed to listen to her coach. I've learned through my black belt journey that we all do.

It was 1998 and I was going through my first divorce. It was completely contrary to everything I believed in—I was definitely of the "'til death do us part" ilk. Yet there I was, in the middle of another argument with my soon-to-be ex-husband. The telephone argument was over my upcoming black belt test. I'd started martial arts three years earlier to have something fun to do with my children. And while their interest had ebbed and flowed, I had fallen in love with the tae kwon do discipline. After training diligently six days a week (even with a torn meniscus), I had passed my tryouts and was ready to tackle the two-day test to earn my first-degree black belt. As I've described in *Finding Our Wings*, it was my first step in reclaiming my power and identity, yet now, I was trembling over a stupid phone call.

"I can't believe you're going through with this!" he had

shouted at me. "If you get hurt, don't expect me to give you any money. I'm not paying for you!" It was hard enough trying to get him to agree to child support and I had no illusions that he would try to help me—despite my having spent 15 years as a stay-at-home mom, managing our finances, tending our home, and raising our three kids. I was going to have to figure it out on my own.

One month after that gut-wrenching call, I sat on the floor of the San José Civic Auditorium. It was evening, and I was exhilarated. I had done it! I had made it through the two days, passing my test with flying colors. In fact, I'd learn later that I had won the Best Technique award in my division. It was grueling—I was bruised, bloody, yet bursting with joy. I'd had more fun than I'd had in ages. My sons James and Alex were in the crowd with a video camera, cheering me on. The day couldn't have been better. Only one thing remained before we went outside for four hours of conditioning.

The brick breaking.

Brick breaking was the only part of the test that wasn't mandatory, yet it was the highlight for many students. My grandmaster took the microphone to invite any tester 18 and over to come to the stage to break a brick, one for each degree of black belt. Instead of jumping to my feet, bursting with the confidence I'd relished all day, I was instantly paralyzed, hearing those harsh words in my head: "I can't believe you're going through with this! If you get hurt, don't expect me to give you any money. I'm not paying for you!"

What if I did get hurt? I'd seen people break their hands breaking bricks. I'd broken plenty of boards, but never a brick. I was suddenly deflated and fearful, my nascent confidence far too fragile to survive the onslaught of the ugly memory. My instructor walked past, looking quizzically at me. "Are you breaking?" he asked. "I-I'm not sure," I stammered.

"Yes, you are," he said without missing a beat. True to my martial arts training, I responded with a "Yes, sir," and stood up quickly. As I walked to the line gathering in front of the stage, I prayed, "Lord, I have no idea what I'm doing. I need your strength. Help me, Lord."

The grandmaster began speaking again. "Breaking a brick isn't a big deal," he said. "It's not something you put on your résumé. Think of it as a metaphor, something you need to break through." He continued, "Maybe you need to break through negative self-talk. Maybe you need to break through a relationship." I was suddenly filled with intense determination.

Give. Me. The. Brick.

I strode onto the stage, full of purpose. I didn't have the faintest idea how to break a brick—I just knew I could... that I *must*. I watched the testers who went before me, using various methods—knife hand, palm strike, elbows. I decided on a palm strike, and I moved into place with the next flight of testers. The noise of 2000 people in the stands vanished. I stared down at the gray rectangle, perched on the cinder blocks—the only reality in my universe. The grandmaster began the count.

One.

Two.

Three.

On "three," I kiyapped loudly and drove my palm through the brick as though it were butter. It was an incredible moment—the only time I cried all day. *Between you and me, God,* I thought, *there is nothing I can't do.*

Even as I walked to the stage, I'd had no idea if I were actually going to break the brick. But my grandmaster's voice penetrated my fear and the fog in my head: "*Use it as a metaphor.*" When I was unsure about even attempting the challenge, my instructor's brief but powerful comment, "Yes, you are," spoke purpose and courage into my heart. His belief in the value of what I was about to do—*and my ability to do it*—was the motivation, the coaching I needed. And by listening to my coach, I overcame my fear and reached a height of confidence I would not have otherwise experienced, no matter what my accomplishments were that day.

Cindy's 7th Degree Brick Break. Photo: Roberto Fernandez II

Each of us needs someone in our corner, someone who believes in us even when we don't believe in ourselves. If you don't have that person, find her! You will eventually grow strong enough to be your own coach, but it doesn't mean you're weak if you need some support in the early days—or months or years. Remember: Babies need help learning to walk, and we all need support to regain our footing after a breakdown. As a Christian woman, I also listened to my heavenly coach: *I can do all things through Him who strengthens me* (Philippians 4:13).

Too many times we hesitate to request or accept the help we need. It's not a matter of abdicating responsibility or being perceived as incapable—seeking and receiving help is essential to our growth. The very best athletes in the world don't prepare and compete alone. They all have teams of coaches to prepare them, support them, encourage them, and occasionally kick them in the rear.

One caveat: Don't just reach out to anyone.

It's important to exercise discernment when allowing people into the private areas of your pain and growth. Keeping it bottled up and private isn't good and neither is indiscriminately sharing. However, be sure you don't use that discernment as an excuse to stay cocooned and not reach out. Just like gearing up to get in the ring, you need to find the coaches who can help build your confidence and strength by telling you the truth...about the glorious and wonderful *you* and all that you are capable of doing and being.

———

It was five black belts later, and I was ready for my third Mastery test. A big part of the 2016 Mastery test was the physique challenge. All the school owners and master instructors competed in age brackets: I was in the women's 50-59 year old group, which had some extremely fit testers. Early that year I had lost a fair amount of weight due to the stress of the layoff and divorce, but a couple of months before the test I determined I would deliberately sculpt my body for me, not just lose weight as a result of my poisonous situation in life.

The day came for us to take photos to submit to our Association for judging and for inclusion in the event program. The program would be distributed on the last day of the test to thousands, both testers and spectators. My ex-husband got the studio camera that I'd purchased and took pictures of all 20 of our Mastery testers. In my photo, it's clear from my expression that I was horribly uncomfortable. In a cropped workout top and booty shorts, I look fit...and miserable. Ever mindful of everyone else's feelings, though, I didn't want to make a scene and took my photos with the rest of the team.

That night in my counseling group, I showed the pictures to my friends. They were aghast. "You look awful," said one, truthfully and not unkindly. The consensus was I looked like hell—and they weren't going to put up with it. The deadline to submit the photos was the next day, so two of them rearranged their work schedules and insisted they meet me at my studio in the morning for retakes. The environment couldn't have been more different from the night before. We laughed and hammed it up for the camera, and they took the photo that garnered me the Best Physique award. A photo that didn't just show my abs, it expressed the joy I felt hanging out and being supported by dear friends—coaches—who just wouldn't take no for an answer.

Had I not listened, I would have submitted a photo that sucked the life out of the entire program, a photo birthed from the "should" side of my brain, the side that didn't want to make waves or make anyone (even a serial adulterer) uncomfortable. Instead, I listened to my coaches—the strong women who believed in me, were proud of the work I'd done, and who wanted to help me showcase my accomplishment. The coaches who simply refused to let me enable the status quo.

Coaches do that. They see what you've achieved and they make a space to trumpet your results. How often do we squelch the urge to publicize our progress? It feels awkward —like we're boasting. We're happy to brag about those we love, but it's very difficult to be our own celebrity spokesmodel. Who of us has been socialized to be overtly confident? *Words are powerful* and we need to speak and hear confident words of truth. Until we are comfortably able to share what we've done with appropriate pride, we must rely on our coaches to push us in this area.

Who is consistently in your corner? Who sees the best in you when you don't see it yourself? Find the person who is willing to tell you the truth in love—who will confront you when you're off base, who comes alongside you with a hug and a word of encouragement when you're down. The one who has the good ideas and the guts to challenge you when you need it. *And the one who will teach you how to speak highly of yourself.*

One exercise I give some of my leadership clients is to write out a list of ten sentences describing themselves. The first sentence is completely benign: I start mine with "My name is Cindy and I have green eyes." Each sentence should get progressively more difficult to speak out loud. By the time I get to number ten, I'm saying, "I am an excellent executive speaker coach and you should hire me to work with your C-suite." That's not easy to say. But it gets easier with practice. In this exercise, I ask my client to read her sentences aloud, looking at someone with whom she feels safe. She then notes at which point she begins to feel uncomfortable and when she begins to look away, or speak less clearly. That's the point where we start working. By repeatedly reading these sentences, we can become more comfortable stating them—they are facts, after all. It's an excellent exercise to desensitize ourselves to the discomfort.

When we have begun to find ourselves after a tragedy, it doesn't take much to derail us. Being fragile as you begin the reclamation work is not bad or weak or small. It's *human*. Reaching out to someone trustworthy—a coach—is the right thing to do. But keep in mind that coaching includes some butt-kicking as well as encouragement. Sometimes we need a stern talking to from someone who loves us and believes in us and knows that we can be more than we are. True friendship doesn't shirk the hard truths that will propel us forward in our path to joy.

BE CAREFUL

As you progress, expect that there may be those who are no fans of yours. We all have people in our lives who find solace in our sadness, some twisted satisfaction in our misery, insecurity, and depression. They are the voices who denigrate or undermine or just chip away at our new confidence. *Expect that there will be people in your lives who need you to stay less than.* Their own damaged self-image depends on you not transcending your tragedy or failure. Finding the coaches who lift us up isn't the only task at this point in our journey: We have to say so long, farewell, auf wiedersehen, goodbye to those who do not truly wish us well.

Cutting off people is hard. It hurts. It feels ugly. It doesn't have to be—we need to be able to speak difficult truths in objective, matter-of-fact ways. A good coach will work with you to practice speaking truth in this manner. It's easy to say "I have green eyes." It's not so easy to say, "I regret that you can't seem to support me in my personal growth. I care about you and I wish you well, but for my own emotional wellbeing, I do not choose to continue our relationship." That can seem well nigh impossible. But what is the alternative? To continue to bear the brunt of another person's brokenness? Are you really going to keep taking those punches?

We have to find the way. It's essential that we surround

ourselves with those who will coach us to success and freedom and joy.

About a year after my second divorce, I received a registered letter in the mail from an attorney. Turns out my ex-husband had been engaged to another woman while we were married and had swindled thousands of dollars from her. She and her attorney were coming after me, making the assumption that I knew about and was complicit in the theft. I was shattered—not because I learned that my ex had been cheating (again), but because I felt utterly and completely idiotic. Moronic. Stupid. You name it—pick the nastiest euphemism for a lack of intelligence and I gutted myself with it.

How could I not have known? How could I have been so blind? Here I was, successful in so many areas of my life and yet had been duped by a con artist. Only one year past my divorce, I was still working to reclaim my identity and strength. After I received the letter, I fell backward, hard.

A dear friend snapped me out of it—one of my Mastery test photographers. Alison is from Louisiana and, as she likes to put it, sometimes this devout Christian woman just "goes Cajun" when the need arises. "He fooled everyone," she insisted. "You aren't stupid—he's just fucking evil." She made me write down an affirmation: "I know Whose I am and I'm a badass wherever I go." The yellow note still sticks on the TV in my Austin bedroom. The juxtaposition of my relationship to God, my "badassery," and her cussing still makes me giggle. But Alison's Cajun coaching was what I needed to remember myself and to shake off the mean girl in my mind—the one who was ready and willing to drag me to the dark place I thought I'd left behind.

A good coach knows your value, your ability, and what you need to achieve your potential. Make it a priority to find one.

ASK YOURSELF

Where do I minimize or refuse to believe the truth about myself?

_____

_____

Who believes in me more than I believe in myself?

_____

_____

What prevents me from seeking genuine support?

_____

_____

Who in my life doesn't support my growth and journey to wholeness?

_____

_____

What prevents me from breaking close ties with those who undermine my emotional health?

_____

_____

No one wins Olympic gold alone. Even the most elite athletes need coaches. So do you.

———

PUTTING IT ALL TOGETHER

As I've described, in 2016 I ran into a brick wall in life. I was going through my second divorce, struggling financially after a layoff, and preparing for my sixth-degree black belt test. Part of the test included a bo form—a series of choreographed moves with a six-foot staff. Bo is not my weapon of choice. I pick nunchucks when I have the option, and I was struggling with the form. It included hand rolls, spins, and throws, and I ended up dropping the staff or hitting myself in the head with it every time I practiced. *Every time*. I began calling the bo "the bane of my existence"—it seemed I would never get the hang of it.

My grandmaster purposely designed the 2016 test to push his school owners and senior instructors to the limit. He told us he wanted us to feel like white belts again...and I certainly did. One week, I was in California on business and

I let him know I'd be in town. He graciously offered to give me a private lesson at his studio in Santa Clara. I jumped at the chance. While the school owners in northern California got to train with him and improve their technique weekly, being in Austin meant training alone without his keen eye.

When I got there, he hugged me and told me to "grab a bo"—ugh! I had hoped we would work on other parts of my curriculum. But there we were and there was nothing to say other than "Yes, sir!"

We worked for an hour on the routine. I think he was surprised at how uncoordinated I was with the bo; I was a fifth-degree black belt, after all. But his generous patience never flagged and when I finally completed a hand roll, toss, and spin in a row, he said, "Let's stop on that note!" He told me not to worry, that I would get it and I would be fine. I wasn't so sure.

When I returned to Austin, I realized what I needed to do. I needed to put myself in a challenging position that would push me to succeed. I also wanted to show my students that their leader went through all the same difficulties they did—that I was humble and ready to learn.

And so I entered the women's black belt weapons form division in the Lone Star Open tournament in Austin, one of the biggest tournaments in the state.

I practiced that bo form hundreds of times. I used different weapons to find the right length and heft for me. I stayed after classes night after night, practicing those hand rolls, spins, and tosses. My goal was simple: go to the tournament, compete strongly in my division, and *don't drop the bo*.

The day arrived and I got to the tournament. I spent most of the day coaching my students in their divisions, cheering and shouting encouragement during their fights or forms competition. And then it was my turn. Black belt division, center stage. Audience surrounding the oversized ring that was elevated for greater visibility. Three senior black belt judges stared impassively at me as I announced my name, school, and form. And then I began.

"Hand roll...behind the back...spin overhead," I whispered to myself as I went through the motions. "You'll be fine," I heard my grandmaster say in my head. And then it was done.

I didn't drop it. Relief and a profound sense of accomplishment came over me.

I got second place—a four-foot tall trophy and the admiration and respect of my students.

This book isn't just a bunch of martial arts stories. These seven steps are truly metaphors for life. I used every one of the steps at the tournament, but I also use them in business, relationships, finances...every aspect of life. My experience at the Lone Star Open was a microcosm of these steps:

Get in the ring: I had to do it. I was knocked down emotionally, relationally, and financially. But I couldn't sit on the sidelines spectating or judging. I had to compete to win.

Get in the right ring: Lone Star Open was a big stage, but I'd been there before and knew what to expect. I didn't enter the black belt men's heavyweight sparring division. I entered the right division for me.

Get prepared: I worked with my grandmaster and I practiced, practiced, and practiced some more. I worked with a variety of different staffs to ensure I had just the right one for my size and strength. I watched a video of one of our senior black belts performing the moves and mimicked them over and over.

Get comfortable with punches: If I were going to succeed at the tournament, I needed to not just show up and hang onto the bo. *I needed to compete.* I went to my ring determined to do my best and to defeat the other women in my division.

Don't fight mad: I recognized and acknowledged that I was frightened. I didn't want to look stupid in front of my students or embarrass myself in front of my peers. I felt insecure over my failed marriage and my job loss. I talked to a select few friends and my counselor and I determined to reframe my thoughts: I was a success because I tried. Because I put myself out there. My students would be the better for seeing me be vulnerable, and that brought me to a place of peace.

Mix it up: I could have entered the tournament and competed with my nunchucks form, something I was far more comfortable with. But I needed to try something new, something that pushed me beyond my comfort zone and proficiency. There was no other way to build the confidence I needed.

Listen to your coach: I am a perfectionist. I hate it, but it's the truth. I can be utterly vile with my self-talk. For the months before the tournament, dropping the bo or hitting myself in the head became an opportunity to not only denigrate my martial arts ability, but to call myself vicious, hurtful names. If I had continued to listen to the toxic voice in my head, I would never have entered the tournament nor passed that part of my black belt test. But I told that mean girl in my mind to shut up—to leave me alone. And I chose to listen to my grandmaster, who told me I could do this...that *I would be fine*. I listened to my students, who were so excited to see me compete. I listened to voices who would encourage, uplift, and support me. *And I defeated the enemy who always seeks to tear me down.*

———

Putting all the steps together allowed me to succeed. I gained a great deal of confidence from my Lone Star Open experience, a template for so many areas of my life. But it wasn't enough to conquer my own fears, insecurities, and inner hate speech. There's another step that brings us full circle, a step that integrity won't allow me to skip.

You see, it's not all about you.

Cindy Earned 2nd Place at the Lone Star Open

RAISING MY HANDS

Section Three

DON'T STOP NOW

At my studio, we have the SWAT program: the Super Winning Attitude Team. When students reach blue belt (the intermediate rank) they can be invited to join the program. These invitations are treasured by students. It's an honor to be selected because the SWAT members have the opportunity to work not as students, but as junior instructors. They lead warm-ups, demonstrate techniques, and generally serve as role models for our younger martial artists. It's a significant part of their leadership training, a component of martial arts (and life!) that too often gets overlooked. When they have advanced and shown both technical proficiency and maturity, SWAT instructors can even work alone on the mat with a small group of students while the senior instructors teach the larger class. To maintain their standing as SWAT instructors, they are required to help out with a minimum of one class per month. As a part of the program, they get leadership training, exclusive hangouts with me and our senior black belt instructors, and a fancy SWAT Instructor patch for their uniforms.

The program is special to my students and it's special to me.

"Samantha" started martial arts when she was still in elementary school. She loved it from the very beginning as a white belt and came to class as often as possible. When she reached blue belt and was invited to the SWAT program, she was eager to accept, teaching far more than the once per month requirement. She enthusiastically participated in the weekly "mat chat" sessions where we would discuss teaching methods and talk about what was working or what they needed help with. Samantha always came prepared with her notebook and pen, taking copious notes, even as a ten-year-old.

One day during our weekly mat chat, I asked if anyone had anything to share about how their teaching was progressing. Samantha's hand shot up immediately. When I called on her, she excitedly described a drill she had found helpful as a beginner and how she was now using it. "My students are really getting the curriculum, ma'am," she told me. "And they're having fun!"

My students.

It was all I could do not to cry. *My students.* In two small words, Samantha made the leap many adults never achieve:

She took what she learned, used it to help someone else, and created happiness and a feeling of accomplishment in those she'd helped. And in so doing, she experienced the joy only a generous moment like that can create. Samantha is now a third-degree black belt and ready for college, but I've never been as proud of her as I was at that moment.

As you put these techniques into practice in your own life, be mindful that there are others who could genuinely benefit from your experiences. So often we isolate when we are in the midst of pain, and we likewise cordon off the lessons once learned. It's as if we take advantage of the lesson and put it in a box, seal it tight, and put it on a shelf in the basement, locking the door behind us. Yet a significant part of reclaiming strength and joy is taking those hard-won trophies and sharing them with someone behind you on the journey. What you've learned from your hardship is only part of the equation: how can you make things a little easier for someone else? Can your experience help another woman shortcut part of her pain?

TOO BROKEN FOR THE RING? LUCINDA'S STORY

I once had an adult student—I'll call her "Lucinda" —who had been severely abused as a child. Lucinda's martial arts journey was slow and painful. Although she progressed quickly through the beginner belts, when she reached the intermediate rank she slowed significantly.

Sparring was a problem.

Grappling was a problem.

The idea of her lying on her back with someone in her guard, putting her in a vulnerable position where she could be controlled, was overwhelming to her. There were plenty of times she nearly quit, her emotions too fraught to continue.

But she was so tired of being afraid. And she trusted me.

During sparring classes, she would work only with me. While the other students would mix and match partners, she and I would work together and I would step by step teach her the techniques while honoring her boundaries. Lucinda was a fighter—she was a powerful, intelligent woman in every aspect of life. But she was traumatized, and the actual physical touching triggered her over and over. Listening to her stories broke my heart, and I was determined to give her what she needed to succeed. I'm not a therapist and I was concerned about putting her through too much. So we slowly, painstakingly, and lovingly worked through the curriculum, giving Lucinda the space to feel and cry and push and fight her fears.

Slowly but relentlessly, she overcame.

The first time Lucinda came to my house to watch UFC fights, she huddled in a recliner with her hand over her face, peeking out from time to time, horrified at the violence. She joined a houseful of my students for "Fight Night"—an evening of mixed martial arts, snacks, and camaraderie. She asked lots of questions, her analytical mind trying to understand what was happening in the bouts, all while her emotions were roiling. Lucinda was passionate about taking control, about having the skills she would need to protect herself from physical attack and the emotional strength to do more than curl up and cover her eyes.

Lucinda is now a second-degree black belt. She earned a Best Tester award at her first-degree exam, performed one of the most badass (yep, I used the word) open forms I've ever seen at her second-degree test, and is an exceptional mentor to younger students. When we watch a UFC bout now, she's shouting at the TV, yelling at the fighters to keep their hands up or other similar encouragements. When we are not watching together, we are typically posting comments back and forth on Facebook about what we see and the fighters we follow regularly. The transformation has been remarkable.

What happened to Lucinda?

She decided to get in the ring. But getting in the ring was so triggering, so fraught with nearly paralyzing fear that she had to take very slow and careful steps to get started. *She listened to and trusted her coach.* When I told her I knew she could do it and I promised to be there every step of the way, she believed me and trusted me. Along the way, she became one of my dearest friends. My experiences were nothing like hers, but by coming alongside her, believing in her, and offering love and support, I was able to help Lucinda overcome.

Sometimes we fight flesh and blood. Other times we fight shadows and memories. No matter what the bout, no matter how bloodied and exhausted you are, there is hope. Finding the right ring and the right coaches can make all the difference. And when you find yourself on the other side, it's your turn. Lend a hand, a heart, a hug.

GIVING BACK

In 2020, it was time for another Mastery test. I originally planned to test for my seventh degree black belt, but had to pull out due to serious osteoarthritis in both my shoulders. The decision to withdraw from the test was one of the most difficult decisions I've made. We train for these moments, and it was an extra special test, because my grandmaster was testing for his tenth degree—the highest rank achievable. Testing with him and our other founder was an honor not normally accorded martial artists. At that rarified level (great grandmaster), the tests are usually held privately and without lower belt ranks—even black belts—in attendance. All of us school owners were deeply honored to be included.

But in September 2019, I reached a crisis. My shoulders degraded so severely that I needed help from my training partner just to put on and take off my uniform top. At one point, I was in San Francisco on business and stopped at

Nordstrom on my way to the airport. I tried on a cute top but then realized I couldn't take it off. There was no way I was going to ask for help from the saleswoman! Trying not to cry in the dressing room, it took me a full ten minutes to wriggle out of the garment—I simply could not lift my arms over my head. It was only then I finally accepted the fact there was no way for me to participate in the test and do it justice. Instead, I had shoulder replacement surgery and grieved the loss of the opportunity.

But I could still teach and prepare my own Mastery students for their rigorous, six-day experience.

And one of the most valuable things I did for them, apart from putting them through grueling training, was to tell them stories. But not just mindless anecdotes: I shared with them the hardships I endured over my three Mastery tests, the lessons I learned, and the truth about what it takes to succeed as a master instructor. They all had their own ideas about what they'd go through. I had experience, knowledge, and wisdom.

And so I shared.

In 2006, I tested for my fourth-degree black belt. It was my first experience with the Mastery test, and I had heard a lot of stories. One year, the testers were dropped off in San Francisco at 9 a.m. with a quarter and an apple—and a requirement to be back in San José, an hour's drive away, by 5 p.m. Another time, they spelunked through tight-fitting tunnels and traversed caverns at the beach. They sat for two hours in a sweat lodge in the Santa Cruz mountains. I had heard the stories before my first Mastery experience but I wasn't well prepared. I had severe arthritis in my knees and couldn't train as hard as I wanted to. By that point, I'd already had three surgeries on my right knee and one on my left. I knew my curriculum well (nothing wrong with my brain), but my body was not in the best shape. I had made a commitment to myself six months previously to reach a certain weight and hadn't even come close. I felt awful.

On the very first day of the five-day test, we weighed in. I started the testing week 12 pounds over my goal weight and seriously doubting my ability. I ended up on a team captained by a woman 20 years younger who was gung ho and hard core. She took her role very seriously and frequently snapped at anyone she felt wasn't measuring up. On that first night, we were graded on traditional forms and I was going hard, feeling like I'd done well. Instead, shortly after we finished that section, she approached me and told me one of our founders felt I wasn't pushing hard enough and to "step it up." She delivered the message coldly—*Would this old broken woman hold back the team?* It was a foreshadowing for the rest of the test. It was miserable.

I was a poor teammate because there were things I just couldn't do. Instead of doing my best at the modified activities and being thankful for what I could do, I was bitter and angry. Even the challenges I could participate fully in were tainted by my lack of preparation and health. Truth is, I was in the wrong ring and I was unprepared. And when I received my new belt at the end of the week, I didn't even want to wear it—I didn't feel I had earned it.

Out of six black belt tests, I have had two really lousy experiences. The stories from those black belt tests are just as important as the stories from the great tests—maybe more so. I'm not proud of those tests. I wish things had been different. But if I refuse to share the lessons I learned during those difficult challenges, I am being stingy with the growth and hard-won education that could help my students achieve their own black belt goals. Likewise, as much as it would be easier to put my life lessons in a box and store it on a shelf somewhere, that's a miserly choice. If I have something that can help another woman and it only costs me a bit of sadness, regret, or a hint of embarrassment, how can I withhold it?

There's an Old Testament story about Moses and the Israelites. They were in a battle against Amalek and Moses stood on a hilltop overlooking the fight. When Moses held his hand up, the Israelites were winning; when his hand dropped, the Amalekites prevailed. The task proved too much for Moses and he was unable to keep his hands up. But his brother Aaron and his friend Hur came to the rescue. They provided a stone for Moses to sit on and they held his arms up as he grew weary. "Thus his hands were steady until the sun set" (Exodus 17:12). Their support enabled the Israelites to win the battle.

LIFTING UP OTHERS: LUCINDA'S STORY

Every one of us has had the experience of simply running out of strength and courage. I have had coaches who supported my arms—through divorce and disaster, through grief and trauma. Good fighters win in the ring. True, generous fighters move to the corner and lift up someone else. Some days, my friend Lucinda couldn't keep her arms up. The weighty and debilitating trauma threatened to overwhelm her. I have lifted my friend's arms and I have watched her generously lift others'.

ASK YOURSELF

What story have you heard in the past that helped you in a difficult situation?

_____

_____

What prevents me from sharing my story and letting my lessons help someone else?

_____

_____

Who do I know who could benefit from hearing my story?

_____

_____

Don't keep it to yourself. Pass it on.

———

WE DESERVE JOY

Learning how to fight has been my liberation. I realize that fighting may be an odd metaphor for this process—this terrifying, exhilarating, difficult, gut-wrenching journey back to wholeness. Some believe that self-care is the answer, but that can devolve into self-absorption. Others advocate a radical altruism that can degrade into martyrdom. I don't assume this method will work for everyone, but I have found true healing through the practice of martial arts— both in my body and in my spirit.

I've realized that genuine, lasting healing *requires reclaiming*. It isn't enough to forgive and move on. By fighting through—by figuratively kicking, punching, and gouging the literal hell out of my life—I've built the physical, intellectual, emotional, and spiritual muscles that allow me to stand up when I'm knocked down. To reclaim the life that I was created to experience, the life of joy we all deserve.

After my second divorce, my therapist wisely recommended that I "reclaim my space." I decided that if I couldn't live at the beach, I'd transform my Austin house into a spa. I bought new bedding—a bright white, puffy comforter and pillow shams. My son and a friend ripped out the ugly 10-foot-long mirror in the bathroom, replacing it with lovely smaller wood-framed mirrors over each sink. I selected the palest blue paint for the walls and gauzy white sheers for the windows of my bedroom and sitting room. With little money but an unwavering commitment to reclamation, my best friend Cathie and I built white IKEA bookshelves and turned the sitting room into a reader's paradise, filled with all my favorite books and vases and vases of blue and white silk flowers.

My Cajun Christian friend—one of the women in my almost-rejected counseling group—asked if she and her husband could help paint my bedroom. I had been dreading the task, but I demurred—that was too much to ask, with the high ceilings and size of the room. But she insisted they wanted to do something kind for me and, one evening while I was at a concert at my church with my goddaughter, they came to my house and painted.

Hours later, I returned from the concert. I walked in through the garage and heard rap music blaring. Puzzled, I walked through the house to the dining room—where not only my friend and her husband sat, but three other counseling group friends and one other husband. They were playing cards, drinking cocktails, and laughing uproariously.

I was stunned. What was going on?

They took me back to my bedroom where the six of them had not only painted the walls, they'd hung the curtains and filled the room with framed photographs of the beach. One gorgeous, huge framed photo of a surfer on a massive wave was mounted above the headboard—a photo from Hawaii, where one of my friends had gotten married. Other photos were from Costa Rica, where another friend had tied the knot on the beach. One friend who hadn't been able to join the party had sent a large pot filled with succulents.

It was overwhelming. I have never in my life felt such love.

Even the best fighters have people in their corner, offering water, coaching, ice for black eyes, and emotional encouragement. Decorating my reclaimed space was simply an expression of their love, an outpouring of generosity and kindness. The love and support of these women helped make the fighting possible. Could I have done it alone? Perhaps. But saying *yes* years before to my counselor's gentle suggestion to "prayerfully consider it" meant I'd taken advantage of the opportunity to build the relationships that would sustain and strengthen me as I flexed my own muscles. A beautiful new bedroom was just the cherry on top of the sundae. Their coaching and love were the rocks I learned to lean on.

Refusing to accept anything less than a beautiful, joy-filled life is only the first step. Like any successful martial artist, we have to commit to growth and progress that doesn't always come easily or feel good. There are always more improvements we can make, challenges to overcome, and lessons to learn. And sometimes, those lessons include humbly accepting the generosity and love of friends. And the results—the brilliant, life-affirming results—are so very worth the investment. Make that investment in yourself and refuse to accept less than what you were created to be. Don't just settle for being happy. Lipstick and shoes make me happy. That's transitory and circumstantial. But love? That brings me joy. And you don't have to be a black belt to deserve pure, unmitigated joy.

ASK YOURSELF

What is the difference between happiness and joy?

_____

_____

Do I believe I deserve to be joyful?

_____

_____

What stories do I tell myself about what I don't deserve? Where did these stories originate?

_____

_____

What would change in my life if I allowed myself to believe I am worthy of joy?

_____

_____

What is one thing I can do today that will bring me joy?

_____

_____

Joy is infectious but it requires nurturing. Give yourself permission and you will be amazed at the results—personally, professionally, and relationally.

———

GRACE

Once we've made the decision to get back into the ring, it would be nice to think all will be well. *I'll practice/rehearse/prepare/whatever in advance and I'll waltz in and take the title.*

But you know it doesn't work that way. Simply making the decision to live—truly live—is never a guarantee that nothing else goes wrong, that we are somehow immune from further disaster. Life isn't scripted and there are no promises that cannot be broken. The challenge is to give grace. To receive grace. To bathe in grace day after day after day.

To do that, we need to be honest. We need to recognize, acknowledge, and name what has damaged us, what kept us out of the ring. What knocked us out, made us tap out, ripped our hearts apart. We have to be courageous in a way that we've never been before. *And then we need to receive the grace that is the balm to our souls.*

You may be fortunate and have a wonderful support system that can show you that grace. But more important is showing it to yourself. When we suffer, how often do we turn it on ourselves? Blame ourselves, bemoan our failure to see and act, tear down our character and intelligence?

We can be our own worst enemy.

One summer, we were visiting family in Fresno, California. I was ten years old, my brother eight. We were roller skating outside at dusk, racing each other down the block. I was on one side of the street, he on the other. We were flying down the sidewalks, glancing across the street, shouting barbs about who was fastest. We were unfamiliar with the neighborhood and weren't paying attention to much other than our race. Too late, I looked up and saw the curb.

I hurtled over the edge and landed hard on the street, just as I remembered the repaving we'd seen earlier in the day. The street was nothing but sharp rocks that shredded the knees of my bell bottoms. The pain was intense and I cried out as my brother skated quickly to my side.

"Sis, are you OK? Oh, man..." he looked at me, wide-eyed. "Look at your knee!"

I looked down and my stomach lurched. Bits of rock clung to bloody shreds of skin.

"Mom's gonna be so mad," he warned.

"Not if no one tells her!" I snapped. "You have to promise not to tell her! She'll scrub it and use that horrible liquid soap stuff." I wiped away the tears and made him promise not to tell our mother. He reluctantly agreed and we skated—me half limping—back to the house. We snuck in through the back door, and I went straight to the bathroom where I picked out the rocks I could and dabbed at my shredded knee. My brother found me a couple of bandages, and I put them on. I changed my jeans and pretended nothing had happened. "With any luck," I said, "she won't notice."

I still have a scar on that knee.

I hid my injury as long as I could until it wasn't possible any longer. Back home in San José, my mom noticed me limping and demanded that I show her what was wrong. I was in so much pain, I finally acquiesced. I hopped up on the counter in the kitchen and she took off the bandages. The wound was full of pus and the skin around it was red and hot. I had only succeeded in allowing it to get infected.

How often do we just wipe down our wounds and slap a bandage on? We feel stupid for putting ourselves in harm's way, for not thinking through the circumstances that led to our injury. We find some way to blame ourselves and we hide from the very things or people who could help us.

And those wounds fester. They fill with pus—with toxic pain that only further reminds us that we made bad choices or that we are somehow responsible for the bad things that happened to us. And then we get scared. We know that by the time we finally acknowledge the poison seeping through us, it is going to hurt like hell to rip off the bandage and clean it out. And so we keep pushing, pretending, punishing ourselves.

By the time I let my mom see my knee, it was bad. She was as gentle as she could be, but she had to clean out the wound. She grabbed the green bottle of Phisohex—the "horrible liquid soap stuff" I dreaded. Even the water running on my knee was pure agony. She took a cloth, lathered it up, and dabbed, then rubbed at the wound. Finally, the blood ran clear into the sink. I was in tears, and I'm certain she was close to it.

My mom got a fresh square of gauze and covered it in Neosporin. She gently laid it on my knee, securing it with tape. She made me promise never to hide something like that from her again.

I wish I could say I honored that promise. Some lessons must be learned more than once.

Far too often we take the punch for others or for circumstances beyond our control. We assume responsibility for things rightfully belonging elsewhere—or simply random events that took us by surprise. Could I have been more careful? Could I have surveyed the landscape before commencing a crazy race with my little brother? Could I have gone straight to my mom after my fall?

Sure. I could have done all those things...*if I weren't a ten-year-old little girl.*

I didn't do anything wrong. Being carefree and careless was my job. But I didn't understand the concept of grace back then. All I knew was that I felt embarrassed and stupid for getting hurt. Every one of my actions after falling stemmed from those negative emotions.

We may not be ten years old, but we are still taking responsibility for things beyond our control. We undermine our value, question our worth, denigrate our intelligence, disregard our skill.

And when we do, we douse our light and rob this world of our talent and our gifts. We warp our trajectory and derail our purpose. It's like fighting with one hand behind our back. We may be able to stand in the ring for a bit like that, but it's not sustainable. If we are truly committed to overcoming trauma and reclaiming our power and joy, it begins with a viciously fierce commitment to truth and an irrevocable devotion to grace.

Grace. The implacable foe of judgment. The unearned favor that stems from unconditional love. My faith tells me that I have it from God. My experience denies it to myself on a regular basis. It is a daily effort to love without judgment, to accept imperfection, to reject shame and insecurity.

To receive grace.

And yet I must, if I am to continue this path to wholeness. I must fight...and I must love.

When I consider my own journey from child to woman, I think back often to those home movies, to the joy-filled little girl I used to be. I've worked hard to find a way back to her, overcoming my challenges, tragedies, and mistakes with a patchwork quilt of ferocious determination and humble learning. It's not easy to climb back into the ring when I'm wounded, but I know staying on the sidelines brings me no closer to joy. Building my *self*—my confidence, abilities, courage, and strength—has meant hard work and sacrifice. It's also brought me closer to faith and peace.

I have to honor that little ten-year-old girl, racing down the sidewalk. I have to remember the three-year-old cherub wearing cat-eye glasses and running laps around the backyard. She's still me. And she still deserves grace.

So do you.

ACKNOWLEDGMENTS

This book began as a keynote at a University of Texas Graduate Women in Business event. I'm grateful to all the students who encouraged me to "write a book!" after hearing the address. Who knew using Pinky and the Brain as a goad for action could be so fruitful?

I'm grateful to my editor, Melanie Spiller, who gets my voice but doesn't let me get away with anything. And to Michelle Morrow, the brains behind the visual expression of my story. I'm thankful both these women nudge me to think bigger about projects and to dream expansively about the future.

To my friend Brenda Rivera, owner of Photography by Brenda and Jabari, who consistently manages to capture the best photos I've ever taken.

My deepest gratitude to the one who's known me

longest and continues to be my biggest fan—my brother James Owen, whose relentless support and love has seen me through both ugly and joy-filled days.

Thanks also to friends who know my story and believed in this project even before I was sure I did. Irene Baptist has been pushing me to write a book for over a decade after hearing me speak at a women's retreat. Julie Rose, who started out as a colleague and became my dear friend, showed me the way, as she stretched her own wings and published three brilliant historical fiction novels. And Cathie Fincannon, my dearest friend who's been there through almost all of the stories in this book, has been my ceaseless cheerleader. I am deeply indebted to each of you.

And to the entire Ernie Reyes West Coast World Martial Arts family: thank you for turning a mom who wanted something fun to do with her kids into a black belt school owner. Special thanks to amazing master instructors and mentors Hector Rodriguez, Diana Sublett, Gloria Telles, and Dennis Woodsmall. My deepest gratitude to Scott Smith, who scolded me so many years ago, "Don't fight mad." Your encouragement and support over the years has made all the difference in the world. To my great grand-masters, Ernie Reyes Sr. and Tony B. Thompson: bless you both for being there throughout my journey, supporting me through training, surgery, divorce, death, and miracles.

Thank you to my students, who regularly teach me new things about being a black belt in life, not just on the mat. It is my honor and privilege to know you and be a part of your black belt journey.

And thank you to my wonderful family. Your love, patience, and creativity spur me to new endeavors every day. This book wouldn't be possible without you.

COMING SOON

DON'T FIGHT
MAD
A Companion Journal

Cindy Villanueva

ABOUT THE AUTHOR

Cindy Villanueva is an author, martial artist, marketing pro, professor, and mom. She is the owner of Ernie Reyes West Coast World Martial Arts in Austin, Texas and the founder and principal of Knockout Marketing Strategies. She is an adjunct professor in the College of Business and Communication at Concordia University Texas, where she earned her MBA. Cindy is the co-author of Finding Our Wings: Seven Entrepreneurs on Reclaiming Hope and Power and is a regular speaker on women in business issues. Cindy has four children and two grandchildren and splits her time between Austin and New Smyrna Beach, Florida.

facebook.com/@CindyVillanuevaAuthor

linkedin.com/company/knockout-marketing-strategies-llc

amazon.com/Cindy-Villanueva

goodreads.com/20555518.Cindy_Villanueva

Made in the USA
Middletown, DE
17 April 2021